The Musée d'Orsay was opened in 1986 in a former railway station designed early this century by Victor Laloux. It brings together works of art from the period 1848–1914, forming the link between the Louvre and the Centre Georges Pompidou. This special edition of *Connaissance des Arts* offers a guide to the museum and its collections: painting, sculpture, decorative arts and architecture.

Cover page:
Claude Monet, The Artist's Garden at Giverny, *1900, o/c 81 x 92 cm (detail).*

1. Interior of the main hall with Hercules the Bowman *by Antoine Bourdelle, 1909, bronze 248 x 247 cm.*

1

PREFACE

By Henri Loyrette, director of the Musée d'Orsay.

When the Musée d'Orsay opened in December 1986, reactions were varied but never indifferent; the interior design by the A.C.T. team and Gae Aulenti was alternately praised and criticised, as were the museological choices made by the curatorial team lead by Michel Laclotte. The upholders of the old-style Manichaeism which divides the second half of the nineteenth century into the Impressionists (the good) and the 'pompiers' (the bad), criticised the 'rehabilitation' of academic painting while their opponents felt it had not been given enough attention. Many voices, however, emphasised the novelty of a project which presented all the arts over a period (1848–1914) of more than half a century: painting, sculpture, decorative arts, photography, architecture, not forgetting the 'exhibition dossiers' which accompany temporary exhibitions, literature, cinema, music, graphic arts and the theatre.

Today, nine years on, our station-museum moves ahead at full steam. The pace is fast: it has received over thirty million visitors, including those who have seen the exhibitions we organise at the Grand Palais. The initial plan has thus proved pertinent and it is clear that it answered a deep-set expectation in both the French public and visiting tourists. Our team has been partially renewed

and has seen the recent departure of Françoise Cachin, director from 1986–1994, but it continues to work to its original plan. Nevertheless, having taken certain initial criticisms into account, and anxious to allow the way the works of art are presented to evolve, some changes have been made. Monographic hangings have been favoured in the Impressionist and Post-Impressionist rooms: in the upper gallery, known as the 'galerie des hauteurs', which opens the 'New Painting' section with the Moreau-Nélaton collection, individual rooms have now been allocated to Monet, Renoir, Cézanne and further on to Van Gogh and Gauguin, with the Bonnard room rounding off the survey of paintings. Architecture and international Art Nouveau have been regrouped in the upper pavilion; the exhibition dossiers, previously distributed around the museum circuit, are now grouped together on the ground floor.

2

2. View of the columned gallery on the upper level of the museum showing The Circus *by George Seurat.*

3. The façade of the Musée d'Orsay overlooking the banks of the Seine.

But above all it is the collections themselves which have developed, this being the primary reason for regular rehangings in all disciplines: examples of new works include Daubigny's *Snow*, Barye's *Tartar Warrior*, Monet's *Le Déjeuner sur l'herbe* and *La Rue Montorgueil decked out in Flags*, Seurat's *The Black Knot*, Gauguin's *Oviri, Be Mysterious* and *Self Portrait with Yellow Christ*, *The Study* by Van de Velde, Gallé's *Hand with Seaweed* and *The Game of Croquet* by Bonnard.

All this, alongside the numerous temporary exhibitions, concerts, cinema festivals, courses and conferences, provides ample material to lure a substantial public to make regular return visits to the museum. It only remains for us to wish these faithful visitors and those who are visiting for the first time, a visit which is thought-provoking, full of discoveries and, above all, pleasurable. H. L

3

4

5

6

FROM RAILWAY STATION TO MUSEUM

In the eighteenth century, the quai d'Orsay, until then an undeveloped area with a few large town houses, became one of the favourite spots of the Parisian aristocracy, marked by the building of the Hôtel de Salm (the Hôtel de la Legion d'Honneur) between 1782 and 1788.

In 1810 Napoleon decided to erect a building there for the Ministry of Foreign Affairs, later allocated to the Audit Office and the State Council. The large edifice, similar to a Roman palace, with heavy architecture and a cumbersome interior design, profited from its decoration by well-known artists, including Théodore Chassériau, who painted his most prestigious large-scale work on the staircase walls, devoted to three allegories, *Peace, War and Commerce*. On the 24 May 1871, at the height of the bloody events of the Commune, the palace was ravaged by fire and the remaining fragments of Chassériau's work were torn from the charred walls and transferred to the Louvre. The Audit Office remained a ruin until 1898, and around it grew an extraordinary wild garden, incorporating the pollen of exotic plants cultivated in the greenhouses of neighbouring residences. The garden is described in the *Revue Illustrée* in 1888: 'Arriving at the burnt-down palace, my friend stops, ecstatic, and admires the surprising vegetation that has grown up in less than seventeen years: brambles, impenetrable even by light, moss covering the pilasters, grass growing thick through every crevice, an impromptu virgin forest whose roots upturn the pavings and break up the stone staircases, lending these new remains the aspect of the most beautiful of antique ruins.'

For more than thirty years the fate of the shell of the old palace remained undecided: would it be possible to restore it and reinstate the building to its original function? This project was quickly abandoned. It was suggested that a museum of Decorative Arts could be built on the site, for which Auguste Rodin received the commission, in 1880, for the *Gates of Hell* (the original plaster of which is now on display in the Musée d'Orsay).

Eventually, in anticipation of the Universal Exhibition in 1900, and in

How the building designed to house Orsay railway station, head of the line towards South-West France from 1900 to 1939, became a major national museum. By Caroline Mathieu.

4. Orsay railway station at the beginning of the century: this old photograph illustrates how the building's original exterior has been preserved.

5. The station in 1900: the building is already characterised by its volume and light.

6. The great clock in the central aisle, thankfully preserved.

FROM RAILWAY STATION TO MUSEUM

response to the requests of the Orléans rail-road company, who stressed the inconvenience of their location at Austerlitz station, far from the city centre, it was proposed that a railway terminus be built. Many people were extremely worried by this idea, fearful that one of the most beautiful sites in Paris was to be disfigured for ever by a noisy, dirty, industrial building. To calm the critics, the Orléans company called upon three respected architects, Emile Bénard, Lucien Magne and Victor Laloux, from whom Laloux (1850-1937) was selected by popular vote in April 1898. Winner of the Grand Prix de Rome in 1878, Laloux had already built the Basilica of Saint Martin, the town hall and the railway station in Tours, his native town. He needed to design a building capable of receiving travellers in large numbers yet one that could be integrated into the heart of historic Paris, that of the Louvre and the Place de la Concorde. To this end the large, industrial structure, thirty-two metres high, made of metal and glass, was masked by an imposing stone façade. The building progressed rapidly, thanks to a system of two teams, a day team of three hundred workers and a night team of eighty, and the station was officially opened on the 14 July 1900. It was the first large modern railway station, designed for electric traction, which explains the luxurious central hall, decorated with sculpted and painted staffs which are reminiscent of the grander Roman baths or Roman basilicas.

Conveyor belts for the luggage, lifts for the passengers, five underground railway tracks, Orsay station, head of the line to South West France, saw, over a period of forty years, the departure of almost two hundred trains a day. The station façade on the rue de Bellechasse and along the rue de Lille housed a grand hotel with nearly four hundred rooms, the splendour of which can be judged by the ballroom

7

7. The façade of Orsay station, on the rue de Bellechasse, c. 1910.

8. The ballroom of the former station hotel. Behind Nature revealed to Science *(1899, coloured marble and onyx 200 x 85 cm) by the sculptor Barrias, is* The Birth of Venus *(1879, o/c 300 x 218 cm) by William Bouguereau: the essence of official art under the Third Republic.*

and restaurant. The decoration of the entire hotel was decided on by Laloux and entrusted to official artists; there were paintings in the departure lounge by Fernand Cormon, in the dining-room by Gabriel Ferrier and Benjamin Constant, and in the reception rooms by Pierre Fritel. The quai façade was decorated with three statues representing the towns of Bordeaux, Toulouse and Nantes by the artists Hugues, Marqueste and Injalbert.

Rapid progress in mechanization soon made the station impractical to use and main-line traffic was brought to a permanent halt in 1939. Laloux's monument, abandoned by the SNCF, was subsequently used for a wide variety of events and occasions. It was the rest centre

for prisoners returning in 1945; Orson Welles's *The Trial* was filmed here in 1962 and, for a longer period, the Madeleine Renaud and Jean-Louis Barraut company set up here; the Parisian auctioneers also made it their home during the rebuilding of the Hôtel Drouot. The station hotel closed its doors in 1973.

In the 1960s there was talk of demolition: 'Laloux's building will be missed by no-one, although built in 1900 it has none of the grace of that period and hides a mediocre metal structure behind its stone façades, heavier than any in Paris.' A luxury hotel was suggested, for which Le Corbusier, among others, produced plans, elevations and models. A first prize was even awarded to the architects Coulon and Gillet, but their project was quickly abandoned. In 1973 - benefitting from a revived interest in the nineteenth century, and saved in sort by the destruction of Baltard's masterpiece, Les Halles, Paris's central market, and the general outcry this provoked - the station was placed on the supplementary list of historical monuments. It finally became a listed building in 1978. It was agreed that a museum should be established, aimed at providing the link between the Louvre and the Musée national d'Art

9. 10. The original architecture and decoration blend harmoniously with the modern renovations.

10

moderne, representing all fields of artistic creation from the second half of the nineteenth century and the early twentieth century.

In 1979, following a competition held between six architects specialized in the renovation of historic buildings, a project by the A.C.T. agency (consisting of Renaud Bardon, Pierre Colboc and Jean-Paul Philippon) was selected. In their project, the three architects gave preference to the entrance on the rue de Bellechasse, organizing the collections along the large hall, opening it up in order to preserve the volume of the space and building up on two sides of a large central aisle using the cupola rooms of the old station. Up above, almost vanishing into the sky, the roof area was converted into a long gallery

FROM RAILWAY STATION TO MUSEUM

THE PARIS OPERA

Models and drawings bring to life one of the most important buildings of the Second Empire - the Paris Opera, the work of Charles Garnier. Winner of a competition organised by the Emperor in 1860 to replace the auditorium in the rue Le Peletier, the young architect, thirty-five years old, still an unknown, won the vote of the Empress Eugenie for his project.
Garnier was able to propose a perfectly adapted solution to a particularly difficult problem. His project deliberately breaks from the austerity of Haussmann's boulevards, lined with tall, regular and rather monotonous buildings, with its exuberant, eccentric and, at the time, often-criticised decoration. This combination of styles borrowed from the past was to become *the* Napoleon III style. But the building's main interest lies in its very structure, visible from the boulevard and accessible to all. Here form expresses function rather than hiding it, which means that from whatever angle you look at it, the Opera looks like... an opera house, with an entrance hall, an auditorium, a rigging loft, scenery etc. Begun in 1862, it was only inaugurated thirteen years later, under the Third Republic. S.B.

where the Impressionists are now housed. Laloux's metal pillars and beams and his stucco decoration were kept throughout, restored and highlighted. The earlier building is still very much present in the structure of the new.

Before the collections could be installed, the design of the exhibition rooms remained to be decided, along with the form of architectural design, the choice of materials and colour, and the style of the museum furniture. For this a second competition was held in 1980, bringing in the Italian architect, Gae Aulenti. She proposed a bold architectural style, capable of standing up to the immense volume of the nave, chosing to harmonize the different galleries by using Buxy stone, a patterned limestone from Burgundy, for the floors and walls. Gae Aulenti went for clarity throughout, emphasizing the original architecture and using the language of polychromy.

Various technical problems arose: the building had to be guaranteed water-tight, the acoustics modified - which was achieved by installing resonators in each of the round windows in the central hall - this vast space 32 metres high and 130 metres long had to be air-conditioned and, finally, the works exhibited needed to be harmoniously lit. Indirect lighting was chosen, being the closest to natural light, with the exception of the sculptures which, it was felt, required a more direct source of light. Finally, restoration was actively carried out to recapture the original luxurious style of the great hall created by Laloux, and to rediscover the colour and brilliance of the ballroom and the dining-room.
The original station was built in two years but it was almost ten years before the Musée d'Orsay was finally opened, since when it has received more than twenty-one million visitors.
Restored to new, the building corresponds exactly to the description given by the painter Edouard Detaille in 1900: 'The station is superb; it looks exactly like a Palace of the Arts...'   C.M.

11. *This scale model (1/100) shows the Opera district in 1914 with its network of Haussmann streets.*

12. *Jean-Baptiste Carpeaux,* The Dance, *1869, stone 420 x 298 cm/ The spirited and smiling dancers decorated the brand new Opéra de Garnier.*

11

12

13

HERITAGE AND TRADITION

Even if the majority of their paintings belong to the first half of the nineteenth century, Ingres and Delacroix are nevertheless represented in the Museé d'Orsay by a few late compositions and above all through the numerous other painters who turned to their example for inspiration.
By Arlette Sérullaz.

For all those wishing to get an idea of the evolution of French painting in the second half of the nineteenth century, the collections of the Musée d'Orsay, which continue and complement those of the Louvre, offer a diverse panorama which provides a true reflection the extraordinary richness of artistic creation at this time. Exceptionally fertile in talent but extraordinarily complex, for a long time this period remained torn between two antithetical aesthetic poles, the Apolline and the Dionysiac, to use the famous Nietzschean formula. 'We shall have gained much for the science of aesthetics when we have succeeded in perceiving directly its continuous development from the duality of the Apolline and Dionysiac; just as the reproduction of species depends on the duality of the sexes, with its constant conflicts and only periodically intervening reconciliations… To the two gods of art, Apollo and Dionysus, we owe our recognition that in the Greek world there is a tremendous opposition, as regards both origins and aims, between the Apolline art of the sculptor and the non-visual, Dionysiac art of music.' (Friedrich Nietzsche, *The Birth of Tragedy*, Basel, 1871; Penguin, London, 1993, p. 14)

The Apolline is Jean-Auguste-Dominique Ingres (1780-1867), the Dionysiac his eternal rival, Eugène Delacroix (1798-1863). Having reached the twilight of his prestigious career, the revered master taught the cult of ideal beauty to the young painters who crowded around him. Meanwhile Delacroix, resolutely solitary, looked for extreme emotion and was less preoccupied with determining the exterior form of human beings and objects, than with reaching a means of expressing the inexpressible and capturing human passion in all its diversity. This memorable antagonism, which the organisers of the Universal Exhibition in 1855 enjoyed drawing attention to by allocating a special room for a retrospective exhibition of these two artists, reappears at the entrance of to the Musée d'Orsay, if one takes the time to look first at 'Monsieur' Ingre's *The Spring* and then the sketch for *The Lion Hunt* by Delacroix, which hang near to one another. Carried away by the sensuous pleasure of painting the contours of a woman's naked body, the old man's hand nevertheless continues to draw an outline which is imperceptible but which leaves nothing to chance. In total contrast, Delacroix freely expresses the ardent impulses aroused in his imagination by the memory of Rubens's *Hunts,* mixing bodies and colours in a daring composition of dazzling colours. In the wake of these two pre-eminent figures of French painting, some artists continued to extol the fine equilibrium of draughtsmanship, while others, anxious to maintain the integrity of the creative act, tried to negotiate a delicate balance between the exacerbation and the control of passion. The first won the approval of the jury at the Salon, the periodical exhibition which the majority of artists had long considered as their supreme objective. The others, more often than not, received only criticism and sarcasm. As is well known, the same opposition, strongly embedded in the critic's mind, engendered categorical judgements on the respective merits of one side or the other.

If Ingres strongly influenced the work of, for example, Amaury-Duval (1808-1865, see *Annunciation*), he was less influential in the case of Théodore Chassériau (1819-1856) who, while never rejecting his master (as is clear in *Tepidarium*), paid homage to Delacroix (which *The Fight of the Arab Horsemen* clearly illustrates). Delacroix's example was followed, in a variety of different domains and subjects

13. Eugène Delacroix, The Lion Hunt, *1854, o/c 86 x 115 cm/ A sketch by the master of romanticism, who here follows Rubens, showing the ardour and violence of brush and palette which were praised by Baudelaire in his 'Salon of 1855'.*

13

15

14

15

16

by Paul Huet (1803-1869; *The Abyss: Landscape*), and Eugène Isabey (1803-1886): it is worth stopping to admire the latter's extraordinary *Temptation of St Anthony,* exhibited in the Salon of 1869. Meanwhile, the lure of North Africa and the Middle-East, familiarized by the Crimean war and the building of the Suez canal, can be found in the work of Delacroix (*Fording a River*) and Descamps, who continued to paint oriental subjects until the end of their lives. Its logical continuation appears in the less prominent orientalist masters, amongst whom Alfred Dehodencq (1822-1882) and Eugène Fromentin (1820-1876) are the best known. Although the themes painted by Dehodencq have often been regarded as the simple reflection of those issuing from Delacroix's fertile imagination, it is worth the trouble venturing the the far end of the hall: *Farewell of the King Boabdil* makes one perhaps reconsider before making so severe a judgement. The next generation, who have a room dedicated to them, continues with similar but more realist subjects, stripping away some of the romantic heroism that was so in vogue

14. 15. In The Angelus *(1858–1859, o/c 55 x 66 cm) as in* The Gleaners *(1857, o/c 85.3 x 111 cm), Jean-François Millet presents a fair and timeless image of peasants, in contrast to contemporary portrayals which were often pitying, idealised or caricatural.*

16. Jean-Auguste-Dominique Ingres, The Spring *(1820–1856, o/c 163 x 80 cm)/Ingres's masterpiece, completed with the help of his students, rapidly became an essential reference for numerous artists, right up to Picasso and Magritte.*

at the time. Revealing in this aspect are *The Falcon Hunt* by Fromentin alongside *Pilgrims to Mecca* by Léon Belly (1827-1877), the *Café at Adalia* by Charles Vacher de Tournemine (1812-1872), and the *View of Laghouat* by Gustave Guillaumet (1840-1887). Guillaumet's extraordinary *Panoramic View of the Sahara* (also known as *The Desert*) makes an interesting comparison with Fromentin's moving *The Land of Thirst*.

There is, however, a major exception: the monumental and bloody *Arbitrary Execution under the Moorish Kings of Grenada* by Henri Regnault (1843-1871), where the rich palette of dazzling yellows and reds shows that this pupil of Cabanel's liked Delacroix's art as much as he did that of Ingres. As was the case for Delacroix, it was the shock of visits to Spain then Morocco that radically transformed Regnault's vision. *The Arrival of General Prim outside Madrid* and *Arbitrary Execution*, placed side by side, show how the new freedom of colour was accompanied by a freedom of form which makes this artist, who died prematurely at the age of twenty-seven, impossible to categorize but fascinating nonetheless.

The influence of Ingres is still alive in the work of Alexandre Cabanel (1823-1889) and Vincent Bouguereau (1825-1905), both very mindful of the elegance of good draughtsmanship. Even if these two artists seem to be continuing a tradition rather than pursuing new directions, it would be a mistake not to stop for a moment to admire

17

17. Jean-Baptiste-Camille Corot, Morning: Nymphs Dancing *(1850, o/c 98 x 131 cm)/Towards the end of his life Corot painted imaginary landscapes often inhabited by nymphs such as this one; he sometimes entitled these works 'Memory'.*

18. 19. Five years after the scandal caused by Burial at Ornans *(1849–1850, o/c 315 x 668 cm) in which he portrayed the inhabitants of this small town in Franche-Comté, Gustave Courbet, the poet of realism, presented his enigmatic* The Painter's Studio: Allegory of Seven Years of my Artistic and Moral Life *(1855, o/c 359 x 598 cm). This monumental painting represents those 'condemned' by the painter or society on the left and his friends, including Baudelaire, on the right.*

the sensuous abandon of the female model who posed for Cabanel's *Birth of Venus*, or *Three women: Flight in the Clouds* that Bouguereau conceived for *The Dance*, one of the panels of the Bartholoni drawing-room. Up until the end of the century, a whole line of painters showed a similar preference for the refinement of line, vying with technical ability without however abandoning poetic expression. *The Meeting of Faust and Margarita* by James Tissot (1836-1902) and the *Cockfight* by Léon Gérôme (1824-1904), are fine reminders of this narrative eclecticism, where memories of Antiquity meet with Germanic inspiration. In this respect, Ernest Meissonier (1815-1891) deserves a special mention, now somewhat

(see page 22)

18

19

19

HERITAGE AND TRADITION

THE SALON

The origins of the Salon date back to the seventeenth century, when the Royal Academy of Arts organised exhibitions of the work of living artists in the Salon Carré in the Louvre. The Salon's importance grew through the nineteenth century. During this period, the possibility of exhibiting depended on the approval of a jury, nominated by the Academy, who made it difficult for certain artists to participate. All however tried to take part, since at the time it was the only means of making oneself known to the public and to potential buyers: the artists' future depended on their success at the Salon.

With its dictatorial organisation, the Salon soon became the domain of tradition, of a certain conservatism, of, in a word, academicism. It presented official art which, contrary to the previous century, became increasingly distant from the more innovatory tendencies. In the 1860s, the gulf separating the academic painters from the avant-garde artists became dangerously wide and, anxious for reconciliation, Napoleon authorized the opening in 1863 of the 'Salon des Refusés', a Salon for works rejected by the jury. Courbet, Manet and the future Impressionists all exhibited there.

Although from 1870 the Salon remained a social event, it contained more and more conservative works of art. It was in the 'parallel' salons, (National Fine Arts Society, the Indepdents, the Autumn Salon), that the works of Cézanne, Van Gogh, the Nabis etc. could be seen, prior to a new era dominated by the galleries.   S.B.

20. *Théodore Chassériau,* Tepidarium, *1853, o/c 171 x 258 cm/The subject of this picture was inspired by one of the thermal baths excavated at Pompeii. A pupil of Ingres and an admirer of Delacroix, Chassériau reconciles in his painting the 'two rival schools of line and colour'.*

ORIENTALISM

The Orient, i.e. the arab-muslim world from Morocco to the borders of the Middle East, real or imaginary, fascinated nineteenth-century artists, from Ingres and Delacroix to Fromentin. From the beginning of the 1830s, painters became travellers, bringing back sketches, drawings and watercolours from their long journeys abroad which they then used as guidelines for more ambitious paintings. The 'inspired' vision of the romantics was, however, rapidly succeeded by the picturesque re-creations of the 'orientalist' painters. What is lost in imagination and aesthetic creativity is gained in iconographic verisimilitude or decorative accuracy.

With *Tepidarium* (1853), Chassériau (1819-1856) succeeds in reconciling two traditions: arabesques in the manner of Ingres mix with Delacroix's rich colours, which

20

express more eloquently Chassériau's sensuality, tinged with idealism.

More realist, Fromentin (1820-1876) paints highly polished hunting scenes, fantasias or arab caravans. In the same period, Tournemin (1812-1872) immortalizes his *African Elephants* (1867) in a dazzling light, while Guillaumet (1840-1887) creates images of the desert which communicate his fascination for those distant, exotic lands (*Prayer in the Sahara* (1863), *The Desert* (1867)). The contemporary public were great enthusiasts of this orientalism which respected the 'noble art' of painting.   S.B.

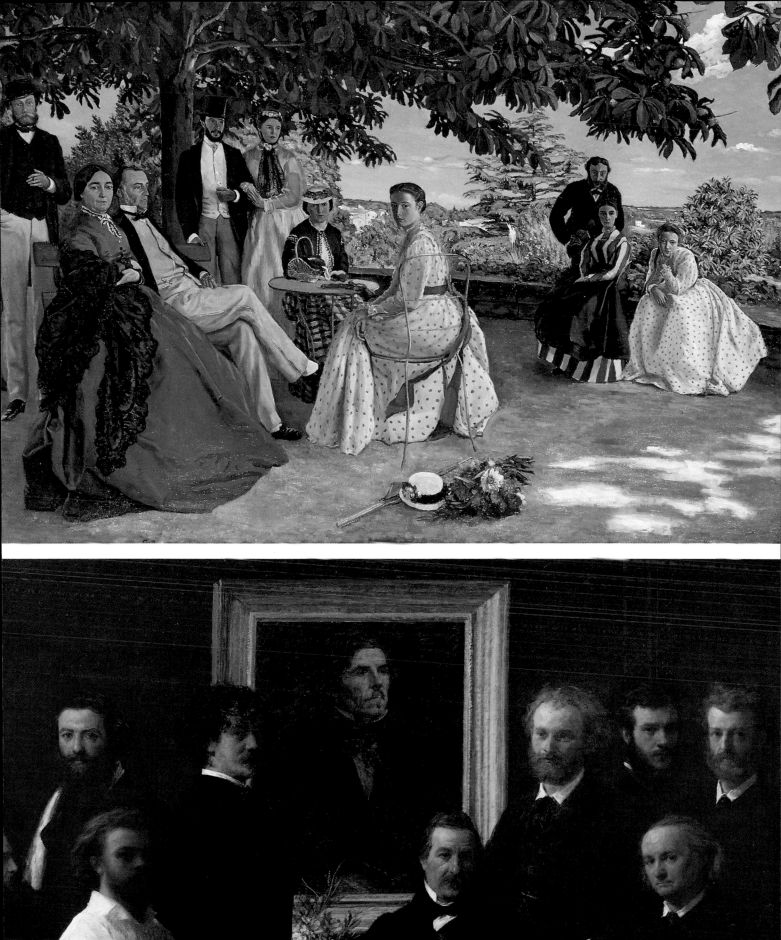

HERITAGE AND TRADITION

21. Frédéric Bazille, Family Reunion, 1867, o/c 152 x 230 cm/This family portrait, shown at the Salon of 1868, combines Manet's influence in the choice of subject and composition, and that of Monet in the sensitive use of light.

22. Henri Fantin-Latour, Homage to Delacroix, 1864, o/c 160 x 250 cm/This painting-manifesto, reminiscent of 17th-century Dutch group portraits, brings together the advocates of the 'new painting' (Manet, Whistler etc.) around a portrait of the master of romanticism, deceased in 1863.

23. 24. In Semiramis Overseeing the Construction of Babylon (1861, o/c 151 x 258 cm), an unfinished painting, Degas refers to the work of Ingres and Gustave Moreau: the hieratic treatment of the figures also evokes the artist's admiration of the old masters of the Quattrocento. An exceptional draughtsman, Degas made numerous sketches (photo below/ Study for Semiramis, 1860–1862, watercolour) before arriving at the final composition.

forgotten, although in his lifetime he enjoyed international renown. His radiant *Riding in Antibes,* shows that beyond his pictures of the Napoleonic era (*The French Campaign, 1814*) and his small interior scenes, Meissonier was also interested in the study of light and should be included as one of the precursors of open-air painting.

The late recognition of Impressionism, has somewhat eclipsed the development of history painting, so active in France between 1850 and 1870: from Henri Lévy (1840-1904: *The Death of Orpheus*) to Gustave Moreau (1826-1898; *Orpheus*), from Jules-Elie Delaunay (1828-1891; *The Plague in Rome*) to Jules Lenepveu (1819-1898; *The Martyrs at the Catacombs*), Puvis de Chavannes and even the young Degas (1834-1917; *Semiramis overseeing the building of Babylon*), subjects taken from Antiquity, from the Bible or from ancient history are not interpreted in a strictly narrative fashion, instead, according to the particular artist, they are tinged with idealism, or indeed symbolism. Thomas Couture (1815-1879) was eager to return to an individual style, working in thick, very light-coloured impasto on a dark brown background which allowed him to achieve dramatic effects in high relief (*Romans in the Period of Decadence*) which his most famous pupil, Edouard Manet (1832-1883) would begin, with difficulty, by imitating.

From the middle of the century, genre painting also went through an important transformation, gradually shedding the low status that it had until then been allotted. Constant Troyon (1810-1865) and Charles Jacque (1813-1894) used enormous canvases to paint cows or sheep grazing (Troyon, *Oxen going out to the Fields: Morning Light;* Jacque, *Sheep Grazing*). Both artists belonged to the Barbizon group - less a school than an independent colony -, which resolutely turned its attention to nature and day-to-day reality. In the 1850s, Théodore Rousseau, Jules Dupré and Narcisse Diaz de la Peña took to setting up their easels in the heart of the forest or in the middle of a field, thus beginning, albeit unconsciously, a decisive revolution in the history of landscape, which was to encourage the rapid development of open-air painting. Meanwhile, certain artists continued, without much self-questioning, in the classical tradition, with works derived from Claude Lorrain (François-Louis Français, 1814-1897, *Orpheus*). Camille Corot (1796-1875), however, elevated this genre to new degrees of lyrical idealisation (*Dance of the Nymphs; Catalpa, Souvenir of Ville-d'Avray*).

With this preference for the natural, the fashion for the portrait, the most constant and most authentic aspect of the genius of French painting, was constantly gaining ground. It was newly encouraged not only by State commissions but also by the new and flourishing bourgeoisie. Whether personal or official portraits, individual portraits or group portraits, all are brilliantly represented in the the Musée d'Orsay. To be convinced, one only has look at *Portrait of Charles Garnier* by Paul Baudry (1828-1886) or *Lady with Glove* by Carolus-Duran (1837-1917), not forgetting the group of portraits by Henri Fantin-Latour (1836-1904), mid-way between Courbet and the American artist Whistler, enveloped in fine ashen shadows, they are the fervent record of the artist's admiration and sensitivity (*The Dubourg Family, Woman Reading, A Studio in Les Batignolles, Homage to Delacroix*). The same Fantin-Latour gives new meaning to still-life (*Flowers; Roses in a Vase*), as does Antoine Vollon (1833-1900) who, following Bovin, combines Nordic stylistic influences with a certain rigour in execution which is entirely Spanish (*Sea Fish*). A.S.

23

HERITAGE AND TRADITION

JEAN-BAPTISTE CARPEAUX

Carpeaux (1827-1875) was an emblematic figure of the nineteenth century whom Edmond de Goncourt described as having 'the fever of a genius in the mind of a marble sculptor'; although much inspired by the art of the eighteenth century, he heralded a revival in sculpture.

He joined Rude's studio at the École des Beaux-Arts, but his master's naturalism and burning romanticism were little appreciated in official circles under the Second Empire and he left him, after which he finally won the Prix de Rome on his third attempt in 1854. In the first work he sent back from the

25

Villa Medicis, *Fisherman with Shell,* the young Carpeaux was paying homage to the *Neapolitan Fisherman* by his former master. With this the struggles with the Academy's restrictive administration began. He was criticised for his independent spirit and was asked to 'elevate his style

by exercising his talent on noble subject-matter. His response was to neglect all the rules. His last work from Rome, *Ugolin,* was meant to illustrate all he had learnt there, yet it fails to comply with any of the established rules: the composition contains several figures and the subject is not taken from mythology. 'A statue conceived of by the poet of the *Divine Comedy* and created by the father of Moses, that would be a masterpiece of the human spirit'.

This circular form of composition would reappear on several other occasions, notably in the bas-relief *Flora* made in 1863 for the pavilion of the same name in the Louvre. At this time Carpeaux enjoyed the patronage of Napoleon III who took his side in arguments with the architect Lefuel. He chose the round again for *The Dance* on the façade of the new Opera House by Garnier - a friend of his since junior school. His group is centred around the Spirit of Dance. Encircled by dancing women, he marks out the steps of a frenzied tarantella on his tambourine. This sculpture provoked one of the biggest scandals of the Second Empire: the critics attacked it in the press and the group was sprayed with ink, after which it was decided that it should be replaced.

His final official commission, the *Observatoire Fountain,* again uses a circular form with its four female figures symbolising the continents. The artist carefully depicts the movement of a foot of one, a leg of another, hands half-open; all three are crowned with flowers and smiling - an

extremely difficult expression to capture: it is the instantaneous which brings Carpeaux close to the Impressionists' study of movement, seizing the fleeting moment. Where in painting a touch of white brings the iris to life, marking the reflection of light, in sculpture, the pupil is hollowed out and a fragment of stone placed in the hollow in order to give an impression of light and volume.

The study of the instantaneous is at its best in Carpeaux's portraits, giving them a rare realism and naturalism. In the bust of *Princess Mathilda*, the tilt of the head, the carnations, the careful working of the eyes and the hair pulled back in a bun perfectly convey the sitter's character. Up close one can appreciate the way the material is used to drape her bare shoulder and how the lace and fur bring out the quality of her smooth skin.

In his portrait busts of the architect Garnier and Dumas fils, the artist was renewing the tradition of busts of artists perfected by Coysevox in the seventeenth century: the loosened tie, open-necked shirt, the head slightly tilted. He brings a touch of modernity in his use of light and the manner in which he sculpts the hair in broad sweeps. In his official commissions - obtained thanks to his friendship with the Emperor, his scandalous looks and his way of assimilating a diversity of influences from the history of sculpture - Carpeaux is a true example of 'fin-de-siècle' eclecticism while at the same time he paves the way for Rodin's modernity.   I.H.

25. Jean-Baptiste Carpeaux, Eugénie Fiocre, 1869, plaster 83 x 51 cm/Reviving an 18th-century tradition, in this portrait of a prima ballerina of the Opera, Carpeaux manages to evoke all the model's elegance and character.

26. View of the central aisle of the museum devoted to sculpture with, in the foreground, Four Quarters of the World bearing the Celestial Sphere *(1867–1872, plaster 280 x 177 cm), project for a fountain by Carpeaux for the Observatory gardens, Paris.*

ART AND INDUSTRY

Designed for large town houses and palaces, or bought at the universal exhibitions of the last century by the great men and women of this world, the furniture and objets d'art in the Musée d'Orsay can only be understood in the context in which they originally came about. As they sit today, isolated like masterpieces on their solemn stands, it is worth situating them, or trying to imagine them, in their original surroundings; they should be thought of as products of a society which begins roughly with the restoration of the Empire in 1852.

The Tuileries and the château of Saint-Cloud, two important examples of the decorative style of the court under the Second Empire, were both destroyed by fire, but certain rooms in Compiègne château and at Fontainebleau, along with a few period documents such as water-colours by Fortuné de Fourier or descriptions given by contemporary critics and journalists, still remain to give us an idea of the type of surroundings chosen by the imperial couple, and more particularly by the Empress. Her taste in decoration was in fact proverbial, and is a good reflection of the fashion of her time: a blend of historical nostalgia with a fondness for comfort. She had always been fascinated by Marie-Antoinette and she created a morbid cult of the unfortunate sovereign, manifest in chapels and private drawing-rooms decorated by Lefuel in a style that has since been referred to as 'Imperial Louis XVI'.

Saint-Cloud and Compiègne retained their eighteenth-century decoration; she added new ornaments (in imitation stone if necessary, to keep up with the times!) to make them correspond to her own idea of her favourite century. In the queen's former bedroom at Compiègne, she replaced the cupids and an eagle by a pair of embracing turtle-doves and bows and arrows, which she considered more 'authentic'. As with her contemporaries, she was not in fact a devotee of the past but was instead only interested is her own perception of it. She did have objects from the former court placed in her apartments (the Riesener writing desk from the Petit Trianon was in her dressing room, Louis XV's desk in her study), but equally, she did not hesitate in having them copied or in commissioning consoles and tables 'in the style of' Riesener or Weisweiler from contemporary cabinet-makers. She had a swing mirror installed in her dressing room which looks as if it could be an original in Fortuné de Fourier's water-colour. However, delivered by a certain Alexandre-Georges Fourdinois in 1855 to the Crown Estates was the following: 'a swing mirror in the style of Louis XVI; mahogany, varnished with rich, carved bronze, mat gilding, etc.'.

The formal furniture, whether old or new, was accompanied by the indispensable occasional or comfortable furniture. Each room had its nest tables and Chiavari chairs, with their structure that defies all rules of design, which performed their delicate ballet around the heavier figures of the other dancers: pouffes, love seats, sofas and armchairs which were generally upholstered in the same fabric as the walls. In order to achieve these interiors, which shamelessly turn their back on the strict distinction we make between 'antique' and 'modern', cabinet-makers and joiners executed endless borrowed designs and inventions without any concern for authenticity. The 'modern' chairs in the card room at Compiègne created by Ruprich-Robert, were designed to make use of Beauvais tapestries from the eighteenth century, while the 'family drawing room' contained chairs designed by Jeanselme in 'a Louis XV style' to be covered with Aubusson's modern tapestries. In the opera house at Fontainebleau

In the last quarter of the nineteenth century, designers, taking their inspiration from styles of the past, used the latest technological inventions to improve furniture and decorative works of art. The Musée d'Orsay's presentation of these masterpieces of eclecticism pays homage to the 'industrial arts'. By Jean-Louis Gaillemin.

27. Henri-Auguste Fourdinois, Renaissance-style credence (1862–1867) in carved walnut decorated with plaquettes of lapis-lazuli and sanguine jasper, ivory- and silver-incrusted interior / This credence was made for the Universal Exhibition of 1867 by the firm Fourdinois; Party, Hilaire and Maigret were responsible for the wood-carving.

there were copies of Jacob chairs, upholstered in the same style as the comfortable contemporary furniture. In 1858, Cruchet provided Compiègne with a centre table and consoles designed to go with the décor of the walls in Marie-Antoinette's old drawing room.

The imperial court, worried about their legitimate right to the throne, preferred the style of the Ancien Régime; Princess Mathilde, who like many financiers of the period liked to see herself as a Fugger or Medici, had a weakness for the Renaissance, while Prince Napoleon set his heart on Greece and Pompeii. There was no contemporary creation that did not quote and reinterpret History, and this with a clear conscience that has long been a source of wonder. The standard formula, which would spread dramatically in the decoration of the Haussmann buildings in Paris, is well known: the entrance was decorated in Courdoue imitation leather, aspiring to the Renaissance, as did the dining-room into which light filtered from an interior courtyard through a few stained-glass windows. The living rooms were Louis XIV and Louis XV, the lady of the house's boudoir Louis XVI and the gentleman's smoking room and study were decorated in a harmony of dark wood which hesitates between a Renaissance and Louis XIV 'Boulle' style. Many questions have been asked about this general fashion in the decorative arts of the nineteenth century for the 'revival' of past styles. First it should be made clear that these 'revivals' did not take place under the Second Empire, but came about under the July Monarchy, as the recent exhibition at the Grand Palais, *The Golden Age of Decorative Arts* reminded us, and as is shown by the 'The Duchess of Parma's Dressing Table' in the Musée d'Orsay which was commissioned from Froment-Meurice in 1845 by women legitimists, supporters of the Bourbon monarchy. It should also be added that a more detailed study of the evolution of styles reveals other 'revivals' in previous centuries, such as the neo-Louis XIV style which appeared around 1760 when a renewed popularity for antiquity was accompanied by a revival of the fashion for Grand Siècle furniture. Designs by Boulle came out of storage, where they had been kept because of their value, and the cabinet-makers of the day such as Levasseur and Montigny made commodes and tables 'in the style of Boulle' which for a long time were thought to be 'Louis XIV'. This latent fashion for revivalism reached its paroxysm in the nineteenth century and this happy concoction of styles was accompanied by a firm belief in the progress of science and industry. It was as if the industrial middle-classes could sense the devastating and nihilistic possibilities of their power, and were trying to exorcise the future and stave off the history that they were in the process of creating. The only real collectors were artists, writers like the Goncourt brothers, eccentrics, bankers like the Pereires or the Rothschilds, or the great misanthropic aristocrats like Lord Hertford. For the industrial bourgeoisie, however, it was out of the question that they should surround themselves with the cast-offs from another age, as this would have been to deny their role as the standard-bearers of modern progress and to acquiesce to the values of a fallen class.

28

28. Max Klinger, Cassandra, *bronze bust, eyes of cornelian, traces of gold on the hair ribbon (50 x 32 x 35 cm)/ A grand expert in polychrome sculpture and in the mixing of materials, Klinger created* Cassandra *in 1886. Editions of the bust were produced by the Gladenbeck foundry from 1900. The red eyes of the prophetess evoke the bloody future threatening her people.*

29. Charles Guillaume Diehl and Emmanuel Fremiet, cedar medal cabinet with walnut, ebony and ivory inlay, decorated with bronze and silver-plated copper (238 x 151 x 60 cm), 1867/ With its Meroveus's Chariot *by Fremiet, this piece illustrates a renewed interest in the use of classical ornamentation inspired by examples from France's past. It was presented at the Universal Exhibition of 1867 in Paris then at the Viennese Exhibition in 1873.*

Neither could they allow any anonymous industrial objects into their homes, since these would not cast a recognised or flattering image on them. They decided therefore, as is indicated in the hybrid term 'industrial arts', to put technical progress at the service of art. Far from being a slave to the past, they appropriated it and infused it with a new life created by the machine. Design and original creation, restricted in the sphere of industry, took hold of the artistic heritage, enriching and improving it. And the designers let themselves be carried away, like contemporary botanists, by the most tantalising grafts which led to the invention of new techniques.

Just as animal species are perfected by change, the marriage of art and industry is renowned for the improvement it brought to the furniture species on the occasion of the great Universal Exhibitions which punctuated the century of industry, from London in 1851 to Paris in 1900. In 1851, at Crystal Palace, the grandiose structure in iron and glass by Joseph Paxton, gardener to the Dukes of Devonshire who had started building greenhouses himself at Chatsworth, France distinguished herself in the diversity of her exhibits, such as the Duchess of Parma's dressing table. The architect Félix-Jacques Duban, the jeweller Froment-Meurice, two sculptors, Jean-Jacques Feuchère and Geoffroy-Dechaume, the industrial designer, Michel Liénard and three enamellers all contributed to the making of this one item of furniture, given as a present by the legitimist women of France to Charles X's granddaughter on the occasion of her marriage to the future Duke of Parma. With its fine ogival arched mirror, its Louis XIV pediment, its rocaille candelabra, its Byantine-arabo-Renaissance ewer and its jewel box inspired by twelfth-century reliquary caskets from the Meuse decorated with little Renaissance bells, to today's visitors it looks, in its heavy glass display case, like a sort of historical dinosaur of the decorative arts, a species which has failed to survive the changing fashions. Nevertheless, the Musée d'Orsay owns a number of specimens from this race of master-pieces including the extraordinary house of Monbro wardrobe, exhibited at the Universal Exhibition in Paris in 1855. It combines a Regency shell with Renaissance caryatids, a Louis XIV mascaron and pelmet with a classic Wedgewood-style medallion; the champlevé and painted enamelwork on copper add an unexpected touch of orientalism. Even more extravagant is Charles-Gustave Diehl's medal cabinet after a design by Jean Brandely, which was exhibited at the 1867 Exhibition and reappeared unexpectedly at Drouot in 1973, when it was wisely bought by the Louvre. With its walnut, ebony and ivory inlay work, its trophies of Gallic weaponry, bull-heads, reptiles and an extraordinary silver-plated bronze relief, representing Meroveus's chariot on the Catalaunian fields, all made by Emmanuel Frémiet, it foils even the most subtle analyses of eclectic furniture.

Displayed in the 'objets d'art' section at exhibitions, the great works of the 'industrial artists' were generally bought by rich amateurs or by sovereigns, either to furnish their homes and palaces (among the most stunning examples are Compiègne, Ajuda in Lisbon and

30. Antoine-Louis Barye, Tartar Horseman (49 x 44 x 27 cm), 1855, patinated bronze partially enamelled and gilded/This work was commissioned by Emile Martin, the director of the Fourchambault foundry. Presented at the Universal Exhibition of 1855, this decorative sculpture was generally sold without the enamelling to a bourgeois clientele.

31. Albert-Ernest Carrier-Belleuse, decorative bowl (44 x 28 x 27 cm), red porphyry, engraved cast silver, porcelain, obsidian, brass/Working with the ceramist Taxile Doat, Carrier-Belleuse wanted to evoke the richness and virtuoso style of Renaissance metalwork.

31

30

ART AND INDUSTRY

Dolman Bache in Istanbul) or to donate them to museums of the 'industrial arts' which were beginning to spring up: the Museum of Manufacture opened in London in 1862, today the Victoria and Albert Museum; and, originally the 'Society for the Progress of Industrial Art' and later the 'Central Union of the Arts', France's 'Museum of Decorative Arts' opened in 1905. These new museums, found also in Berlin, Vienna and Budapest, were generally the product of private initiative, in other words they were financed by patrons of industry who were wary of placing their best models, antique and modern, at the disposal of their workers. Instead, once in the museums, electroplating meant they could be copied and Christofle published catalogues of these reproductions, in which Suger's medieval vase might be illustrated alongside Henry II's armour.

This concern for education led some industrialists to set up evening classes or private schools in order to spread the practice of design through the various domains of industry, and it was the catalyst for a series of 'retrospective' exhibitions designed to make the best productions of the past centuries better known so that the old techniques might be rediscovered and even improved upon. In Jules-Claude Ziegler's workshops the technique of salt-glazing stoneware was rediscovered from German Renaissance models. Charles-Jean Avisseau closely followed the processes used by Bernard Palissy for glazing pottery and Reiber revived the metal patinas and inlays found on Japanese objects. Finally, vital to the war, technological inventions were encouraged and rewarded financially. The 1851 Exhibition saw the rapid development of iron and zinc casting, which meant bronze could be imitated, and Thonet's curved wood and the apogee of papier-mâché, put to every use imaginable. The old and sometimes abandoned gold and silverware techniques were also revived and benefited from new electrochemical gilding. Over the course of the century, the development of electroplating meant that any object could be reproduced and bronze could be imitated, by-passing the engraving stage. In cabinet-making, the band-saw made it possible to achieve veneers as fine as cigarette paper and steam-operated planers facilitated all the mouldings. New techniques making fabrication easier appeared in the domain of ceramics (the Siemens kiln, the use of coal, new casting processes) and in glassware (acid engraving and enamels), which led to new formal inventions. Some disgruntled people resented these improvements, which were too often seized upon by the manufacturers in order to sell at lower prices and spread 'bad taste' through the public. But this diffusion of luxury, or rather of apparent luxury, on all levels of society was part of the original challenge. The tone was set by the Emperor himself when - the story is famous - he ordered a plated 'silver' service in order to make a saving for the State's coffers. But he was also encouraging industrial processes which placed objets d'art within the reach of all pockets, thus opening up new markets and challenging the competition. In the marriage of art and industry, it was industry who brought the dowry and controlled the household budget. J.-L. G.

32

32. Ferdinand Levillain, Diogenes, covered vase (40 x 18 cm), 1891, copper gilt, reproductions gilded and electroplated/A sculptor and medal maker, Levillain used the most modern techniques to create his objects which owe a great deal to his knowledge of Antiquity and the Renaissance.

33. Emile-Auguste Reiber, objects drawn and executed for the Christofle company under the mark 'Christofle & Cie'. A pair of candelabra (56 x 31 cm), c. 1872, galvanised bronze and copper, patinated and gilded, blue enamel and polychrome cloisonné enamel. Sea-horse candlestick (27 x 12 cm), c. 1869–1870, copper, polychrome patinas. Jardinière (13 x 32 cm), c. 1878–1880, galvanised patinated copper/Reiber was one of the promoters of Japonisme in France, borrowing oriental forms and adapting their techniques for industrial fabrication.

33

THE CONQUEST OF MODERNITY

From the mid-nineteenth century, young artists began to overturn the traditional rules of painting. From Realism to Impressionism, from Courbet to Manet, Degas and Monet, Marina Ferretti-Bocquillon retraces one of the greatest adventures in the history of nineteenth-century painting.

34. Gustave Courbet, The Cliffs at Etretat after a Storm*, 1870, o/c 133 x 163 cm/When Courbet painted this powerful seascape, the future Impressionists had already begun painting sites along the Normandy coast. From 1868–1869, the cliffs at Etretat inspired several well-known paintings by Monet, one of which is in the collection of the Musée d'Orsay.*

34

35

36

The Triumph of Nature

From the beginning of the Second Empire, nature triumphed at the Salon and the landscape artists from the Barbizon school, known as the 'glorious generation of 1830', enjoyed a wide reputation and were appreciated by critics and the public alike. The greenery of the Ile-de-France had replaced the Italian landscape in the hearts of the painters, many of whom preferred the noble oak trees of Fontainebleau forest to the golden horizons of the Roman countryside. The majority of them were already painting their landscapes on large canvases, comparable in size to history paintings, and they exhibited them at the Salon.

Théodore Rousseau was one of the leading artists of the French school and his landscapes their pride. Charles-François Daubigny soon caught the attention of Monet; his friends who painted around Barbizon were already benefiting from commissions and state purchases. In 1851, the French state bought Corot's *Morning: Nymphs Dancing*. Four years later they commissioned Constant Troyon's *Oxen going out to the Fields: Morning Light*, where the artist had no hesitation in painting a flat landscape four metres long, the only figures a cow-herd and herd of oxen, silhouetted against the dawn.

Conservative Realism

Rosa Bonheur, one of the most talented and important artists of the Second Empire, was commissioned by the museum of Lyons for her famous *Ploughing in the Nivernais Region* in 1849. This vast canvas full of light is another illustration of work in the fields. The artist contrasts the strong team of oxen with the small peasant 'fixed to the earth' where he struggles knee-deep in mud. The picture is a Georgic celebration of effort, work and permanence which corres-

35. Jean-François Millet, Shepherdess with her Flock, also known as The Great Shepherdess, 1863, o/c 81 x 101 cm/More than simply a peaceful depiction of rural life, this picture, exhibited at the Universal Exhibition of 1867, has as somewhat mystical atmosphere, created by the halo of light surrounding the young shepherdess, the simplicity of her attire and her meditative mood

36. Narcisse Diaz de la Peña, The Heights of Le Jean de Paris (detail), 1867, o/c 84 x 106 cm/Diaz began to paint at Fontainebleau after meeting Théodore Rousseau. In this work, much admired by Bazille and Renoir, Diaz concentrates on the play of light in the greenery of the forest.

37. Charles-François Daubigny, Snow, 1873, o/c 90 x 120 cm/This picture was painted the year before the first Impressionist exhibition. The energetic distribution of colour on the canvas is unusual for the artist. In an account of the Salon, Max de Montifaut compared Daubigny's snow to 'a bit of plaster spread out with a palette knife'.

37

ponds to a type of rural representation strongly promoted at this time. The serene image of the countryside approved by Louis-Napoleon Bonaparte was considered more reassuring than the clearly less docile image of the inhabitants of Paris. As in medieval manuscripts, the rural world was used to evoke permanence, the unchanging rhythm of working in the fields, bound to the rhythm of the seasons, to time immemorial.

Realism, which since 1848 had focused on everyday life and subjects accessible to all, also exploited these rural images. However, country life, also the subject of highly successful novels by George Sand, was often more idealised than real. Hébert's work acquires its languid exoticism from the supple bodies and dark eyes of the Italian peasant women and Jules Breton was quick to realise that an idealised vision of rural life attracted the public, little fond of the harsh description of the misery of the countryside. The beauty of the peasant women in *Calling the Gleaners Home* (1859), and their noble stance make them comparable to modern caryatids. They are radically different to the pitiful gleaners painted by Jean-François Millet two years earlier.

This conservative realism is picked up in the fashion for urban genre scenes depicting widows and orphans. Octave Tassaert's *The Unlucky Family* (1849) or Isadore Pils' *Deathbed of a Sister of Charity* (1850) and Hugues Merle's *Beggar Woman* (1861), both bought by the State straight from the Salon, appealed directly to the bourgeois sentimentalism currently in vogue. As modern, realist versions of the traditional representation of the theological virtues, Faith, Hope and Charity, they did not threaten the established social order. Alexandre Antigna's *Corpus Christi* (1855), is a synthesis of the aims of this realist imagery. The artist choses to reconcile country and city by bringing urban and rural children together, united by faith and a respect for tradition.

38

Official and self-righteous naturalism continued to spread under the Third Republic, but from now on it remained secular. Paintings by Bastien Lepage or Léon Lhermitte celebrated the moral values of the age: merit, effort and work. In the 1880s, naturalism travelled to other western countries and among the most interesting new practitioners were the Belgian painter Léon Frédéric, the Italian Giovanni Segantini and the American Winslow Homer.

Millet and Courbet: 'Socialist Painters'

Millet's approach to the reality of peasant life and Courbet's rural, working-class world were at first fiercely rejected. Although close to their friends of the Barbizon school, Millet and Courbet were more interested in social reality than in the representation of nature. In the Salon of 1850, where Millet exhibited *The Sower* and Courbet *The Stone Breakers*, they emerged as socialist painters.

The epithet does not really fit Millet, even if *The Gleaners*, exhibited in the Salon of 1857 irresistibly provokes La Bruyère's famous description: 'One can see a few shy animals, male and female, dispersed through the countryside, black, livid and burnt up by the sun, fixed to the soil they dig...'. The sketchily painted faces, the low foreheads, heavy jawbones and open mouths all communicate the degradation of the gleaners. The artist was criticised for the dull-witted expressions of his heroines and his muddy palette. On top of this the glaring disproportion between the gleaners' small harvest and the vast haystacks visible on the horizon made the public uncomfortable. But the artist was from a family of affluent farmers who were strong believers and he tended to give his figures dignity and grandeur with a biblical emphasis, the hallmarks of romanticism.

38. Jacques-Joseph Tissot, Portrait of Mlle L.L. also known as Young Woman in a Red Jacket, 1864, o/c 124 x 99.5 cm/Tissot, like Degas later on, saw in the portrait genre an opportunity to depict modern life. The model's simple pose in a familiar universe and her face characterised by an 'unusual individuality' which 'stops one in one's tracks', as remarked the critic Paul de Saint-Victor, combine to give this picture its contemporary feel which was soon to bring the artist success.

39. Edouard Manet, Lola de Valence, 1862, o/c 123 x 92 cm/The Spanish dancer, Lola Melea, also known as Lola de Valence, inspired Manet to paint this portrait in the manner of Velázquez. Baudelaire, among others, was captivated by the picture: 'Among all the beauties one sees everywhere/ I understand, friends, that Desire is sometimes hesitant/ But in Lola de Valence shines/ The unexpected charm of a pink and black jewel.'

MODERNITY

His work gained recognition in the 1860s and the painting *Shepherd watching his Sheep* won him a first-class medal in the 1864 Salon. Three years later, in the Universal Exhibition of 1867, Jean-François Millet was given an official retrospective.

It was Courbet more than Millet who remained the champion of provocation and the target of the critics. In 1851 his work *Burial at Ornans* earned him a scandalous reputation. This vast composition in black and white, highlighted by a very occasional burst of colour such as the red of the priests' robes or a pair of blue stockings, presents an uncompromising gallery of portraits. At first glance the painting seems artistically coarse due to the austerity of the faces, justified nevertheless by the circumstances and by the rugged appearance of the villagers enacting the scene. Courbet became known as the 'painter of the ugly' and since no moral discourse seemed perceptible in the work, it was seen as a 'painting of the void'. Even if the subject of a Catholic burial is distinct, the artist's critical intentions remain far from clear. What seemed shocking at the time were the immense dimensions given to a painting illustrating a banal event in the life of Ornans, and the crude realism of the provincial portraits.

Courbet created a new scandal in 1855 with *The Painter's Studio: A Real Allegory*, an ambitious composition, it too nearly six metres long. Apart from the complicated intentions of the artist which led him to paint the contradictory 'real allegory', the canvas presents a relatively classic composition, modulated by zones of light and shadow. Here too dark tones and black dominate. The sombre colour scheme is barely disturbed by a few patches of light, like the luminous body of the model or the discarded pink dress. Manet would remember this when he painted *Déjeuner sur l'herbe*, where the even more startling brightness of Victorine Meurent's body stands out and the naked woman's clothes bring their flash of colour to the composition. As for Courbet's voluptuous bathers, fleshy rustic nudes closely associated with nature, they were to provide inspiration for Renoir's first nudes.

Courbet: Hero of a Generation in Search of Truth

Courbet's work influenced a whole generation of painters who decided to paint the world as they saw it, making themselves the 'poets of modern life'. Their noisy participation in the salons and their independent exhibition organised on the fringes of the Universal Exhibition in 1855, were to make a lasting impression on artists in search of the new.

What is known as Vagrancy, painted by the young Alfred Stevens in 1855, uses an austere bitonal palette with a few miserabilist touches which hardly prepare one for the elegant pictures of the healthy bourgeoisie which would make him his reputation. *The Two Sisters*, exhibited by Tissot in the 1864 Salon is modified version of *Young Ladies on the Banks of the Seine*, the special atmosphere of which is recaptured in the light filtering through the trees. Carolus-Duran was paying homage to *The Wounded Man*, Courbet's magnificent self-portrait, when he painted *The Convalescent* in 1850, one of the most striking manifestations of a talent which would wither away, like Tissot's, in recording the world of high society.

Fantin-Latour's honest effigies have a borrowed solemnity which characterises *Burial at Ornans*, from where *An Honourable Fine* by his friend Alphonse Legros also takes its inspiration. Théodule Ribot's realism reveals his admiration both for Courbet and for Spanish painters. Manet, however, had no other masters and it was in fact the Impressionists who would interpret this 'reality', so sought after, with the detachment necessary for the rendering of the modern world.

40. Eugène Boudin, The Beach at Trouville, *1864, o/c 26 x 48 cm/Elegant ladies in their crinolines on a beach in Normandy: the contemporary subject lends itself well to a beautiful, atmospheric study. Like his elder, Monet would soon begin to paint fashionable out-of-town resorts: Sainte-Adresse, Trouville and Honfleur.*

41. Edouard Manet, Moonlight on Boulogne Harbour, *1868, o/c 82 x 101 cm/This nocturne following a 17th-century Dutch tradition was painted by Manet in the summer of 1868 which he spent in Boulogne. The moonlight allows the artist to produce rich harmonies in black and white, colours he favoured, highlighted by the mute brilliance of blue or pink. In the hands of the 'terrible realist' who so alarmed the public and critics, a scene from modern life takes on an unexpected and mysterious tone.*

Manet: a New Vision of Modern Life

A pupil of Thomas Couture, whose artistic eclecticism is evident his vast decorative work *Romans in the Period of Decadence*, as is his preference for bright colours and his brilliant technique, Manet chose to practise an art without grandiloquence and to avoid stereotypes. From the outset, his vision of the real was direct and unbiased: he would be neither a history painter like his teacher nor a politically engaged painter like Courbet. The portrait of his parents exhibited at the Salon in 1861 was given much attention by the critics who were either shocked or seduced by the disarming honesty of this young artist's work.

Already apparent in this early work is Manet's characteristic vision, an accurate and detached observation of the world around him, and his preference for black-and-white compositions with touches of colour. The colourful skeins and balls of wool spilling out of the basket anticipate the bright, deliberate rendering of Olympia's bouquet. Meanwhile, the austere faces and the sombre tones dominating the work stem directly from the realist tradition. Manet, like Couture, declared his unfailing admiration for the old masters, but it was to Courbet and the Spanish painters that he owed his search for truth in painting. To them also he owed his preference for compositions in black and white, a preference shared by his friend Whistler, who in 1871 painted a portrait of his mother in 'an arrangement in black and white'.

Divided between his admiration for the old masters whom he wished to equal and his love of modern subject-matter, Manet generally endeavoured to give a modern interpretation of the great classical

42. Edouard Manet, The Fife-Player, *1866, o/c 161 x 97 cm/Manet gives the contemporary sitter a dignity reserved up until now for more illustrious figures. The radical simplicity of the layout, the masterful organisation of colour and the thick brushwork give the picture its surprising modernity.*

43. Manet the Impressionist, On the Beach, *1873, o/c 59.5 x 73 cm/Here the painter substitutes his usual abrupt planes of colour with a style closer to that of his friend, Monet.*

Following double page:
44. Edouard Manet, The Balcony, *1868–1869, o/c 170 x 124.5 cm/Modern majas, the artist Berthe Morisot and the violinist Fanny Claus pose with the landscape painter Antoine Guillemet. The painting was bought by Gustave Caillebotte who bequeathed it to the State in 1894.*

45. Olympia, *1863, o/c 130.5 x 190 cm/Fallen from an improbable Olympia, Venus shows her purchasable body with cold detachment. Manet invented the modern nude which created a scandal at the Salon of 1865.*

46. Le Déjeuner sur l'herbe, *1863, o/c 208 x 264.5 cm/ In the* Salon des Refusés *in 1863, this painting was still entitled* Bather: *Manet follows Courbet in his realist depiction of the nude. But despite her discarded dress and insolent gaze, the bather, modelled by Victorine Meurent, remains a studio nude, distinct from the more sketchily painted background.*

43

themes: *Lola de Valence*, a Spanish dancer, replaces Goya's marquesses and duchesses; *Déjeuner sur l'herbe*, at first entitled *Bather*, modernizes elements taken from Raphael and Titian; with *Olympia* the *Venus of Urbino* becomes a prostitute with an aloof stare; *The Balcony* is a Second Empire, Parisian version of Goya's *Majas on the Balcony*, and the wonderful *Moonlight on Boulogne Harbour* brings up to date a theme greatly favoured by Dutch artists in the seventeenth century. Manet the 'terrible realist' was clearly fond of old master painting. These works, which so shocked the somewhat conservative art lovers at the time, show both Manet's

44

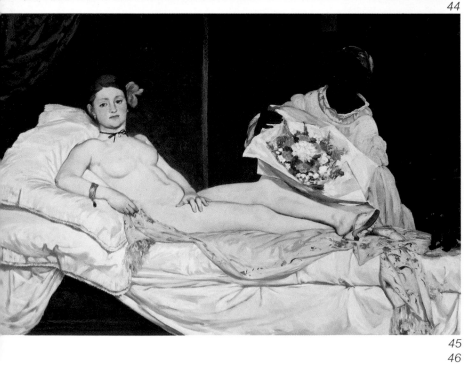

45
46

44

predilection for black and his 'magnificent prune juice' much envied by Degas. The skilled use of black which gives the red and gold *Fife-Player's* uniform all its brilliancy would also catch Matisse's attention, for it is in the *The Fife-Player* that Manet captures fully the art of 'precision and simplicity' that he was looking for. Its effect is of a striking modernity.

The rejection of the *The Fife-Player* from the 1866 Salon provided Zola the occasion to take his stance openly in favour of Manet in the pages of *L'Evénement*: 'I do not believe it possible to obtain a more powerful effect using more simple means...'. From this moment on, Zola would vehemently defend the new painting, created by young artists who followed the side-roads around the Via Manetia: referred to as realists, actualists or naturalists, they were also known as the 'Batignolles school' after the district in Paris where Manet had his studio.

Degas: a Dazzling Gallery of Contemporary Figures

It was in front of a painting by Velázquez in the Louvre that Manet first met Degas in 1861. With their education and tastes in common, friendship came naturally and a strong bond soon formed between the two precursors of the 'new painting', despite their radically different temperaments. Degas, like Manet, loved classical painting while remaining a passionate observer of the modernity of his own era. He too was looking for a new means of expression which would make possible the representation of a society in the midst of radical changes. Finally, he was, like Manet, obsessed with truth. When he paints his nudes in the 1860s there are still references to history painting but he prefers a cruel 'war scene' with contorted bodies and flowing hair to the straight-forward classical Venuses. His rape scene is after all no less credible than the spectacle created by Manet in his *Déjeuner sur l'herbe* of a naked woman having lunch on the grass in a forest clearing. These wonderfully painted nudes prefigure Degas's bathers. These too are pretexts for drawing women in a wide variety of poses: bent over or stretched out, lying, seated or squatting. Curiously these un-usual compositions went unnoticed by the critics in the 1865 Salon. All the stares and sarcasm were instead directed at the insolent *Olympia* by Degas's friend Manet.

It was through his portraits that Degas first began to paint scenes of contemporary life. In *Family Portrait*, where he paints his Italian cousins the Bellelli family, the mother's proud reserve and the father's badly-disguised hostility tell the difficult story of the frustrations and disillusionment of a couple whose only meaning together is given by their young daughters. Despite the numerous references inspiring the artist, the canvas does not look like anything other than a Degas. As a portraitist, Degas avoids the conventional compositions and

47. Edgar Degas, The Bellelli Family, *1858–1867, o/c 200 x 250 cm/In this group portrait of his aunt Laure De Gas's family, Degas observes with a restrained, incisive and fair eye, which he would soon turn onto dancers and musicians, financiers and jockeys, compiling a very modern gallery of Second-Empire portraits.*

48

48. James Abbott McNeill Whistler, Arrangement in Grey and Black N° 1 *or* The Artist's Mother, *1871, o/c 144.3 x 162.5 cm/Bought for the Luxembourg Museum, Paris in 1891, this work was the first American painting to enter the Louvre in 1925. Whistler was a friend of Courbet and Fantin-Latour. This work is one of his masterpieces.*

48

instead seeks out the exact look or pose that will reveal a person's character or a general atmosphere. Initially he made himself the subject of this uncompromising analysis, leaving the image of a tense young man, an admirer of Ingres (*Degas with Crayon Box*, 1855) who then loses his stiltedness during his stay in Rome with a portrait in which he gives all the self-confidence that he himself lacks to his friend Evariste de Valernes (*Degas and Evariste de Valernes*, 1865). But he also paints his close family, his grandfather with his attentive, demanding stare or his favourite sister, Thérèse. Under his brush, the portrait is quickly transformed into a scene of modern life. In *The Orchestra at the Opera* Degas choses to paint his friend Désiré Dihau, a bassoonist, in his professional environment, just as he would later chose to paint Ernest May, a financier and collector, at the Paris stock exchange. The importance given to the background in these portraits upsets the traditional focus on the sitter: modern man is becoming less distinct from his surroundings.

Degas's early works are characterised by precise drawing, matt tones, a preference for contrasting black and white and unusual viewpoints, where the artist does not hesitate in cutting off a head or a leg and showing up an incongruous detail such as a cello scroll or the sombre ballet of eight dancers reflected in a mirror. Degas rapidly cultivated a passion for contemporary life, taking from it a wide variety of motifs such as women ironing or café scenes. But above all it was the dancers (who appear on points in *The Orchestra at the Opera*) whom he observed untiringly, along with horses and women bathing. Gifted with an insatiable curiosity, he produced pastels and engravings, reinvented the monotype and even explored sculpture which allowed him to capture the poses of his favourite models in three dimensions.

49. Edgar Degas, The Orchestra at the Opera, *c. 1870, o/c 56.5 x 46 cm/Although this is in fact a portrait of Désiré Dihau, a bassoonist in the orchestra of the Opera and a friend of Degas's, the picture appears more like a scene from modern life. Degas, even more than his artist friends, tended to blur the different genres of painting.*

50. Honoré Daumier, Crispin and Scapin, *also known as* Scapin and Silvestre, *c. 1864, o/c 65.5 x 82 cm/The theatre stage, with its exaggerated expressions, colours and violent lighting, becomes here the pretext for a caricatural, almost expressionist vision.*

50

Monet: Celebration of the Open Air

From 1865 Monet also contributed to the advancement of the new painting. Contrary to his elders, he was not particularly interested in either classical painting or museums. Following the example of his first teachers, Jongkind and Boudin, he preferred the open air. At first interested in figure painting, he started boldly on a version of *Déjeuner sur l'herbe* almost seven metres long, in order to succeed where Manet had failed before him: the uniformly bright figure of Victorine Meurent seemed artificially imposed onto the landscape behind her. He painted a contemporary picnic using those close to him as models - his future wife, Camille, his friend Bazille and the 'master'

(see page 53)

HONORÉ DAUMIER

Honoré Daumier (1808-1879), referred to by Balzac as the Michelangelo of caricature, was also a draughtsman, a sculptor and a remarkable painter. He left behind him a considerable number of engravings, and above all, lithographs, the majority of which were published in Philipon's journals, *La Caricature* (1830), and *Le Charivari* two years later. A satirical chronicler of the political and social climate of this period, he recreated for the public the theatre of society, whose main players, individuals or social types, were brought to life in his caricatures and sculptures (though the latter, it is thought, were never intended as exhibition pieces). Daumier used the sculptures as models for his numerous lithographs (over 4.000): a sketch was made from life and the main portrait was then executed from memory, first fixed in clay then drawn onto the stone. Using this process, made fashionable by the sculptor Dantan, Daumier not only made fun of his sitters' physiques, but also of the artificial poses they themselves adopted. He was much inspired by the world of theatre, and his painting reveals an unusual use of light; the harsh spotlights on the 'actors'' features brought these 'expressionist distortions' to the canvas before their time. Daumier was a great master and was recognised as such by certain Impressionists, notably Monet, Degas and Van Gogh. S.R.

51

52

53

54

55

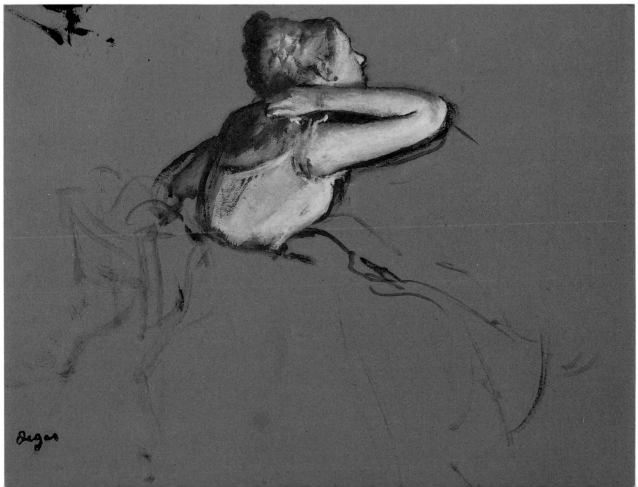

56

Courbet - and an ingenious play of light and use of blue shadows allow his figures to blend into the landscape. The unfinished painting was left to gather mould in a cellar belonging to the artist's landlord. With *Women in a Garden* the challenge was finally met and from this moment on the young Monet was at the forefront of the new painting. In the same year, Bazille painted a family reunion for which he gathered his parents, brothers, sisters and cousins who pose as if for a photographer on the terrace of the family home in Méric. The blinding light of the South of France clearly defines the contours of the landscape and everyone has taken shelter from the sun in the shade of a fig tree. Naturally Bazille had in mind both Monet's *Déjeuner*, for which he had posed the previous year, and *Women in the Garden* which he had just bought. But in this ambitious group portrait there

Previous double page: Three images of women as seen by Edgar Degas
51. Edgar Degas, In a Café *also known as* Absinth, *c. 1875–1876, o/c 92 x 68 cm/Degas, as is his habit, looks at his contemporaries with an analytical eye.*

52. Women Ironing, *c. 1884–1886, o/c 76 x 81.5 cm/On a visit to the artist's studio, E. de Goncourt described Degas as 'speaking their language, explaining the different ironing techniques: the pressured sweep, the circular sweep etc. . . .'*

53. The Tub, *1886, pastel on card, 60 x 83 cm/The bold composition is offset by the delicate lighting and depiction of the model.*

Another favourtie subject-matter, the races:
54. Edgar Degas, The Parade (Racehorses in front of the Stands), *c. 1866–1868, peinture a l'essence on canvas-backed paper, 46 x 61 cm/The matt effect of the* peinture à l'essence *(oil and turpentine mix), the silhouettes standing out from the background, the insistent presence of oblique shadows and the void around which the pictorial space is organised give this racing scene a surprising modernity.*

55. Edgar Degas, Two Dancers Resting *or* Blue Dancers, *c. 1898, pastel, 92 x 103 cm.*
56. Seated Dancer, *1873, pastel and turpentine sketch on paper, 23 x 29 cm/Degas was particularly innovative in his use of pastels, mixing them in new combinations: with oil to obtain a richer effect, with turpentine for a more matt surface.*

57. To achieve greater realism, Degas dressed this Young Dancer at Fourteen *(1879–1881, bronze, 95.2 cm) in a tutu and ribbon.*

57

are traces also of Manet: the distinct contrasts, the expression of a certain solitude which isolates the figures and even the wool basket prominently placed on the small table.

Unlike his friends Manet and Degas, Monet was interested in landscapes. Leaving Gleyre's studio, he dragged his friends Sisley, Renoir and Bazille to Fontainebleau forest and started out as a member of the Barbizon school of painters. *Chailly Road* clearly lies within the realist landscape tradition, giving the impression of nature as stable and unchanging. But with its bold composition and bright tones, this painting reveals a different sensibility to that of Théodore Rousseau or Daubigny. Monet, who grew up in

(see page 56)

58. Claude Monet, Le Déjeuner sur l'herbe, *1865–1866, o/c left hand side 418 x 150 cm, and central section 248 x 217 cm/The theme of the 'déjeuner sur l'herbe', the modern equivalent of pastoral scenes and idylls, allows for a combination of figure and landscape. Monet's painting is a response to Manet's* Bather *painted two years earlier, which also became known as the* Déjeuner sur l'herbe.

58

54

Le Havre, observed the transformations of the Normandy coast which gradually became a very fashionable Parisian holiday resort. In his canvases painted in ever brighter colours, Monet records the grand façade of the Roches-Noires hotel at Trouville, the flags flapping in the wind and the light-coloured dresses of the elegant ladies on the promenade. In winter it is the snow which provides the pretext for bright, luminous colours. *The Magpie*, a magnificent crisp, snow-covered landscape, reflecting the pinks, blues and yellows of the morning light, gives ample

59

59. Claude Monet, The Magpie, *1869, o/c 89 x 130 cm / This is one of the artist's most spectacular winter landscapes. Monet plays with the various effects of sunlight on the snow-covered landscape.*

60. Poppies, *1873, o/c 50 x 65 cm / This painting, exhibited in the first Impressionist group exhibition, sums up all the qualities of Monet's work during his Argenteuil period: a preference for landscape and open-air painting, lively colours, a bold technique and energetic brushstroke.*

61. Sketch for Figure in the open-air: Woman with Parasol turned to the left, *1886, o/c 131 x 88 cm / In 1886, Monet returned to figure drawing after several years of neglect but soon after abandoned it for good.*

60

proof of the artist's originality. Monet was already proving himself a master and showed an inventiveness which far surpassed the sensible compositions by the delectable Boudin.

The Franco-Prussian war and then the Paris Commune mark a pause in the development of the new painting. Degas and Manet signed up and Bazille was killed, never to know the term Impressionism. Monet and Pissarro, however, took refuge in London where they met Paul Durand-Ruel. He bought and exhibited paintings by Manet, Monet and their friends, no longer obliged to submit their work to the fearsome Salon jury in order to make a name for themselves.

(see page 61)

MODERNITY

62

63

62. Claude Monet,
The Garden at Giverny,
1900, o/c 81 x 92 cm.
63. The Waterlily Pond:
Harmony in Green, *1899,*
o/c 89 x 93.5 cm.
64. Blue Waterlilies,
c. 1916–1919, o/c 200 x
200 cm/Monet dedicated the
last twenty years of his life to
the exploration of his garden in
Giverny, a world of greenery,
lyrical, fluid and blue, created
by the artist himself.

65. Claude Monet, Rouen
Cathedral. Main Door, Morning
Sun, Harmony in Blue, *1893,*
o/c 91 x 63 cm/The Rouen
Cathedral *series had a great*
impact on Malevich and the
Haystacks *were a revelation to*
Kandinsky: Monet's series
opened the way to abstraction.

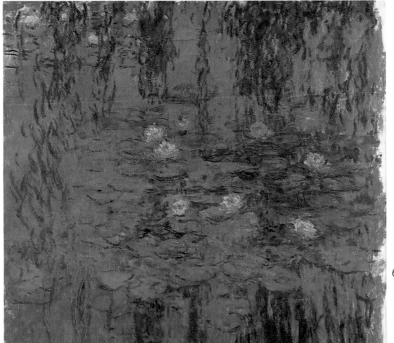

64

58

60

Argenteuil: the Heroic Years

In 1871 Monet settled in Argenteuil where his friends often came to visit him. He was attracted by the lively character of the place which had by then become more or less a leisure ground for Parisians. He painted nearly one hundred and seventy five canvases when he was there which remain among the most striking pieces of his work. He gradually moved away from the figure and turned to nature, more fluid, more animated, more colourful. His style became more detached and more rapid, allowing him to capture the moving image of the sail boats or the reflections of the sunlight playing on the surface of the water. At the first independent exhibition organised by the group in 1874, it was the title of one of these canvases, *Impression: Sunrise* which was to be at the origin of the term 'Impressionism', too simplistic perhaps, but certainly promised a bright future. Manet's family home at Gennevilliers was not far and he often paid neighbourly visits to Argenteuil to see the man he amicably nicknamed the 'Raphael of the water'. Like his friend he abandoned the distinct compositions of the previous years and for a while painted less clearly defined, sketchier forms made with a shorter brushstroke. It was during this period that he executed a very sensitive portrait of Mallarmé in which he captures with startling precision the intimate atmosphere of their conversations and the natural pose, the intelligence and the pensive expression of the poet.

It was during this happy period from 1872 to 1878 that the cohesion of the group was at its strongest. Pissarro, Sisley and in particular Renoir visited Monet in Argenteuil and their canvases reveal how closely they were working together. Sisley was also a passionate observer of water and its reflections, and his paintings remain the closest to Monet's. Yet the rustic landscapes, the village views and the workers in the fields painted in Auvers by Pissarro and Cézanne are also clearly related to these works.

Monet, Sisley, Pissarro and Cézanne may all have favoured landscape painting for a while, but the majority of the members of the group continued, like Manet, to paint the human figure. *Dancing at the Moulin de la Galette* is one of Renoir's most ambitious works, a journey to a modern, Parisian Cythera, where the careful composition is eroded by the flurry of colours and light. From scenes of entertainment in Montmartre, to the more bourgeois elegance of *Madame Charpentier* or *Madame Darras*, not forgetting his voluptuous nudes, it was above all the figure that continued to interest Renoir.

Berthe Morisot and Eva Gonzalès, Manet's talented pupils, depicted young women and children in scenes of everyday life. Mary Cassat, the American artist who admired Degas above all, painted like him in a clean, matt, incisive style and she too preferred figure painting, as did Caillebotte whose originality is apparent in *Planing the Floor*. Caillebotte combined naturalism and modern life with a talent that is

66 Alfred Sisley, Flooding at Pont-Marly, *1876, o/c 60 x 81 cm/For Sisley, the flood provides a perfect occasion to paint water and its reflections.*

67

67. Camille Pissarro, Red Roofs, Corner of a Village, Winter Effect, *1877, o/c 54.5 x 65.5 cm/This picture entered the national collection through the Caillebotte bequest. It illustrates the close relationship between the work of Pissarro and Cézanne.*

66

too often eclipsed by his generosity or his flair for collecting. This work, like many others, supports Degas's argument (he was dissatisfied with the term 'impressionist' which he felt did not apply to him) that the group exhibitions should be turned into a 'realist salon'.

1880-1886: the Break-up of Impressionism

From the beginning of the 1880s the Impressionist group was in crisis. Its members had been united by a common goal: to invent an objective means of expressing modern life. But the battle was long won and most now wanted to follow new, more individual paths. Monet went through a difficult period in Vétheuil, mourning the death of Camille and troubled by financial problems. His move to Giverny brought happier days, a new family, success and travel and he threw himself into new experiments. In the two versions of *Woman with Umbrella* he returned to the figure and large format canvases. But the Giverny patriarch was a constant innovator. In his 'series', the subject of the composition is gradually eroded through its repetition, giving colour an unprecedented force. At the turn of the century, Monet completed the installation of his water garden, and the final two decades of his life were dedicated to the exploration of this world of flowers and water, blue, green and pink, the invention of an artist who, without admitting it to himself, had reversed the Impressionist

68. Gustave Caillebotte, Planing the Floor, *1875, o/c 102 x 146.5 cm/This major work by Caillebotte, gift of the artist's family through the intermediary of Renoir, shows the originality of the artist's realism and the influence of photography on his work.*

68

69. Auguste Renoir, Dancing at the Moulin de la Galette, Montmartre*, 1876, o/c 131 x 175 cm/One of Renoir's Impressionist masterpieces, formerly in the collection of Gustave Caillebotte. Despite the fluttering effect created by the specks of colour and light, the composition is carefully organised according to traditional models.*

approach to painting. Until now Monet had looked for his subject in nature, but here he had composed every element of a landscape consistent with his artistic credo, the pretext for vast, gestural works of ever-increasing lyricism.

Renoir, on the other hand, who since 1881 had declared his 'burning desire to see the Raphaels', finally set off on a long tour of the Italian museums. On his return his paintings were more structured with more clearly defined outlines. They appear as a startling reminder of classical order after the rapid, iridescent and supple works of the previous years. Renoir also turned his back on the alluring mother-of-pearl tones he once used, still visible in *Dance in*

(see page 66)   69

63

MODERNITY

70. *Auguste Renoir*, Dance
in the Country, *1883, o/c*
180 x 90 cm.
71. Dance in the City, *1883, o/c*
180 x 90 cm/Suzanne Valadon
is the model for
Dance in the City *while the*
plump Aline Charigot, later
to become Madame Renoir,
modelled for Dance in the
Country. *Once again Renoir*
takes up the theme of the
dance, but uses a more formal
composition and line.

71

the City, favouring a crisper technique for *Young Girls at the Piano*. From 1907 he spent more and more time at Colettes, his house near Bagnes. From here he wrote to Durand-Ruel, telling him that he had since some time taken up 'the soft and light painting' of the eighteenth-century masters: 'Fragonard, but not as good'.

As for Cézanne, he settled in the South of France in 1878. Tired of the general hostility provoked by his works, he decided that he would no longer participate in the Impressionist exhibitions. In truth his art had never really expressed the fleeting moment, the fluidity of a changing world. Alongside Pissarro he was already trying to express a certain permanence, solid and geometric. From 1878, *L'Estaque* illustrated his desire to 'make something solid of Impressionism, like museum art'. Working alone, his art developed

72

72. Paul Cézanne, Woman with Coffee Pot, *c. 1890–1895, o/c 130.5 x 96.5 cm/Going beyond Impressionism, this painting heralds the figures painted by Picasso and Braque from 1910 to 1914. Cézanne appears here as the 'primitive of a new art'.*

73. Auguste Rodin, Man Walking, *1877–1878, bronze 213 x 161 x 72 cm/ By eliminating the head and arms of* Saint John the Baptist Preaching, *Rodin gives the torso and legs an unusual presence and thus communicates the body's movement with a striking forcefulness.*

towards a more profound lyricism where the Mediterranean land-scape is gradually reduced to an inextricable network of short, oblique brushstrokes. He created a new way of representing space through colour which gives his paintings their astonishing cohesion. In 1886 the last exhibition of the group sounded the final bell for the history of the Impressionists as a group. Monet, Renoir, Sisley and Cézanne did not show their work in this 'eighth exhibition of paint-ing'. Pissarro did exhibit but had already adopted the neo-Impressionist technique of Seurat and Paul Signac. As the history of Impressionism drew to a close, the story of Post-Impressionism was just beginning.   M. F.-B.

AUGUSTE RODIN (1840-1917)

Nature should be shown as it is, in its true state, with an emphasis on the external features of its internal spirit. 'I accentuate the lines which best express the spiritual state that I interpret' (Discussions with Paul Gsell).

This sums up Rodin's work. and is how his sculpture *Saint John the Baptist* came about. One day, a model slightly coarse but full of life appeared at the artist's studio. He posed, placing his weight evenly on both legs, like a pair of compasses. The idea came to Rodin immediately: 'Saint John the Baptist, a man of the earth, of enlightenment.' In 1880, with this work, Rodin achieved a certain fame which had until then eluded him. Rejected from the Beaux-Arts and the Salon, he earned his living working for Carrier-Belleuse as a stone-mason on building sites in Paris. When war broke out in 1870, he took refuge in Brussels, from where, in 1875, he travelled to Italy via Reims, a journey which explains his principal influences: Gothic sculpture and Michelangelo. Inspired by this master of the Renaissance, Rodin's *Saint John the Baptist* became the *Man Walking*: neglecting the arms and head, the energy is concentrated in the *movement* of the legs and the material. Far from the academicism of the period, his model is turbulent, marked the perpetual and agitated movement of the artist's hands. It was clay Rodin felt most comfortable with, it seemed nearer to the earthly life he wished to express, and it is in his bronzes that this quest and life's fragility are most eloquent.   I.H.   73

68

SYMBOLISM

A general trend against positivism and realism, Symbolism brought together a multitude of different artists who were drawn by the mysterious world of dreams and the imagination. By Isabelle Husson.

74. 75. Pierre Puvis de Chavannes, Summer, *1873, o/c 350 x 507 cm, and* Young Girls at the Seaside, *1879, o/c 205 x 154 cm/The entire art of Puvis is contained in these two works. The atmosphere evoking antiquity, the classical inspiration, the monumentality of the figures, the flattening of the surface, the pale, matt colour scheme, the decorative effect and the timeless character of the composition–all imbue these two paintings with a mysterious poetry, which is both serene and melancholy.*

SYMBOLISM

The history of Symbolism belongs to the last thirty years of the nineteenth century; the movement was at its apogee between 1885 and 1895, when its painters became involved in new theoretical ideas.

The Symbolist movement remains one of the hardest to define in the history of art. The variety of its techniques, styles and exponents, and the diversity of artistic, literary and poetic styles only add to the confusion.

In the realm of painting and sculpture, Symbolism refers to an interest in the imagination, the strange, the interior world of dreams. In France, two artists are recognised as the precursors of Symbolism, Puvis de Chavannes (1824-1898) and Gustave Moreau (1826-1898). Puvis de Chavannes places his figures in serene, simple surroundings, while, in contrast, Moreau excels in the mysterious and in an abundance of detail. However different their works, both artists were motivated by an aversion to academicism and realism. In rejecting naturalism, they were aiming to introduce a mysterious and unreal dimension into painting. They shared an admiration for fifteenth-century Italian painting, like the English Pre-Raphaelites, and they both inherited the romantic style of Théodore Chassériau. Puvis de Chavannes particularly admired Chassériau's frescoes, painted for the Audit Office (no longer extant), which inspired his interest in mural painting. *Summer*, painted in 1873, on display at the entry to Orsay, was commissioned by the State for the Musée de Chartres. It belongs to a line of large serial decorations executed by Puvis de Chavannes for various public buildings (the Musée d'Amiens and the Musée de Marseille; the Panthéon; the Palais des Beaux-Arts in Lyons and the Hôtel de Ville, Paris). They include monumental figures which evoke the Golden Age, Arcadia or simply mankind in harmony with nature. There is no action and no apparent subject-matter in the decorative panel, *Young Girls at the Seaside* (1879), just three girls beside the sea, united in serene harmony: the same woman is represented in the three ages of life. The bluish tone and the limited palette evoke an atmosphere of melancholy. Puvis de Chavannes becomes more Symbolist with *The Poor Fisherman* (1881), where he rejects the classical rules of perspective. Depth is suggested in the layering of foreground and background, but there is a certain ambiguity in the poses of the figures: the child, wrapped in its red blanket, seems both to be sitting and lying; the fisherman standing in his boat seems to be crushed both by poverty and by the overbearing landscape. The overall effect is unsettling and adds to the work's emotive charge, its power of suggestion. This painting has its origins in the symbolism of Millet's peasants and in the permanence of their gestures.

76

76. Winslow Homer, Summer Night, *1890, o/c 76.7 x 102 cm/ The sea was the favourite subject of this American artist, who was born in Boston but lived in both Paris and England. The moonlight and the Chinese-shadow silhouettes give this small painting its symbolist tone.*

77. Gustave Moreau, Orpheus, *1866, oil on wood 154 x 99.5 cm/ Praised by Huysmans, Moreau was the French symbolist painter par excellence: this picture, bought by the State in 1866, shows the technical mastery–the colour scheme, the effects of solidity and transparency–of this artist who was to become the teacher of the future Fauve painters.*

While Puvis de Chavannes synthesizes painting and gives it a dry, matt tone, Gustave Moreau prefers refinement and detail. *Orpheus* (1865) represents the perfection of the artist's style, with its enamel painting and glazes similar to a Leonardo *sfumato*. The work is a meditation on death. A silent dialogue is spoken between the young girl, eyes half-closed, and the closed expression of the face of the dead young poet, placed on the lyre. The two turtles at the bottom of the picture represent eternity and the mythical origins of the lyre - the body of the instrument was originally the turtle's shell. Moreau's paintings are like riddles to be solved. Zola writes: 'Moreau paints his dreams, not simple, naive dreams like our own, but dreams that are sophisticated, complicated, enigmatic.' Gustave Moreau referred to himself as the 'worker-builder of dreams'. Admired by the Symbolist writers, *Orpheus* was bought by the State for the Palais du Luxembourg at the Salon of 1866. It was to be the only Symbolist painting exhibited in a Parisian museum until the end of the nineteenth century. Moreau passed his quest for the expression of dreams and emotions on to his pupils at the École des Beaux-Arts. His lessons led to the Fauvism of Matisse, Marquet and Manguin, and to Rouault's religious expressionism. In placing the accent on man's interior desires, Moreau also became an important influence on the generation of 1880: 'Inspiration is never in the subject, it is in the artist's soul; the material used is unimportant.' The artist most receptive to the work of Gustave Moreau was Odilon Redon. His fascination for the infinitely small stems from his master's concentration on detail. His art developed along a different path from academic norms and contrary also to Impressionism. Using engraving and charcoal, he rejected colour, as in his *Black Series* where he attempted to reach an essential truth. His first collection of lithographs, *In the Dream* (1879), presents a world of fantasy. This he inherited from Goya, who, a century earlier, had said: 'The sleep of reason gives birth to monsters'. *Buddha* (1906-7) evokes his fascination for the religions of the East. Huysmans described Odilon Redon as a shadowy neurotic, suffering from hallucinations, transcribing a world born out of illness and delirium. The painter illustrated the works of Baudelaire and Mallarmé, both identified by Jean Moréas, writing in the Figaro in 1886, as the true representatives of Symbolist literature. The Symbolist manifesto of the arts appeared in 1891, in the *Mercure de France*, and was written by the journalist Albert Aurier, who defined its principles in reference to works by Van Gogh and

78. Sir Edward Burne-Jones, The Wheel of Fortune, *1883, o/c 200 x 100 cm/The influence of Botticelli and Michelangelo on this great English Pre-Raphaelite can be seen here in the fine lines of the female figure and the depiction of the recumbent male figures, evoking the famous 'slaves' in the Louvre.*

79. James Ensor, Lady in Distress, *1882, o/c 100 x 80 cm/Whether considering carnival masks or a bedroom interior as here, Ensor always shows the same anguish, precursor of a certain kind of expressionism.*

79

SYMBOLISM

Gauguin. The role of the artist was no longer to imitate nature but to 'visualise' dreams.

Thanks to numerous reviews published in Paris (*Le Décadent, Le Mercure de France*), Symbolism's most creative ground was in France. But in the climate of the Universal Exhibitions and the Salons, there were numerous exchanges between the various Symbolist groups in Europe (London, Brussels…). The Salons played a particularly important role, especially the Société Nationale des Beaux-Arts, founded by Puvis de Chavannes, Rodin and Meissonier in 1890, which regularly invited artists from abroad and actively supported all Symbolists. Eugène Carrière exhibited there, the 'literary painter', a friend of Verlaine's, whom he painted in 1890. Marie-Auguste Ménard also participated. She painted large compositions which recreate a dream-like antiquity, as in *The Golden Age* (in the Law Faculty of Paris University). Influenced by Puvis de Chavannes' image of an ideal world, Henri Martin (1860-1943) evokes, in *Serenity* (1899), a society of druids in a sacred wood. The 'Salon of Roses + the Cross', organised by the eccentric critic, the Sar Péladan (Joseph Péladan), first took place in 1892 at Durand-Ruel's. Lévy-Dhurmer (1865-1953) exhibited there, alongside Osbert Alphons, Carlos Schwabe (1866-1926) and Fernand Khnopff (1858-1921), nicknamed by the Sar (the 'magi' in Persian) Péladan, the 'Flemish Gustave Moreau'. Jean Delville (1867-1953), another exponent of Belgian Symbolism, also exhibited at the Salon of the XX and the Salon of Roses + the Cross. His work, *The School of Plato* (1898), now hanging in Orsay, was originally a sketch for the decoration of the Sorbonne. This Belgian Symbolism in some respects heralded the expressionism of James Ensor.

In Great Britain, Sir Edward Burne-Jones (1833-1898) belonged to the second generation of Pre-Raphaelite painters. This movement, founded in 1848, declared its rejection of the real and its admiration of works dating from the dawn of the Renaissance, before Raphael. W.H. Hunt, J.E. Millais and the Rossetti brothers were the principal members of the group. Burne-Jones was their direct descendant, as can be seen in the ideal, nostalgic beauty of the women in *The Wheel of Fortune* (1883). Alongside them, William Morris transformed their symbolist ideals into a social plan, the Arts and Crafts movement.

The Symbolists opened a new road in painting by introducing the subjective. Painting was no longer a window open onto the world, but a visualisation of dreams, a 'path leading to the interior' for Mallarmé, an 'interior necessity' for Rainer Maria Rilke. Charles Morice refers to it at length: 'Art… is essentially subjective. The appearance of things is only a symbol and the role of the artist is to interpret it. Things have only a truth within them, they have only an internal truth.'

These new criteria for artistic sensibility exposed the psychology of the artist, his inner soul. Towards the end of the century, Symbolism was echoed in literature and in the work of Freud and Jung. Symbolist painting, the externalisation of the individual imagination, is interpreted, however, as having a more universal message. In Huysman's *A Rebours* (1884), the hero, Duke Jean Floressas des Esseintes, an admirer of Gustave Moreau and Odilon Redon, has as his motto: 'Anywhere outside of this world.' This standpoint made him the spokesman of an entire generation.

Symbolism evolved along numerous different paths and influenced the development of several new artistic trends in the twentieth century.   I.H.

80. Odilon Redon, Apollo's Chariot, *1905–1914, pastel on paper 91 x 77 cm/*
Redon's work seems to escape any rational analysis: profoundly independent, mysterious, fantastic, his art is addressed exclusively at the world of the imagination, like an invitation to a dream.

75

THE AVANT-GARDE ERA

The Impressionists exploded the pictorial conventions passed down from the Renaissance and created a new era of the avant-garde: from then on official art, the home of outdated academicism, faced the opposition of a wealth of new forms of artistic expression which explored the formal and expressive qualities of colour. Working alongside the main movements such as Neo-Impressionism, led by Seurat, the Pont-Aven school, initiated by Gauguin, or the Nabis, some prominent artists escape classification: Cézanne, Van Gogh, Redon and Toulouse-Lautrec were among those who lived on the edge of the principal trends which mark the end of the nineteenth century. They cleared the path that would lead to the aesthetic revolutions of the twentieth century. By Antoine Terrasse.

81. Paul Cézanne, L'Estaque, c. 1878–1879, o/c 59.5 x 73 cm/Cézanne portrays a feeling of space, light and air by working with intense areas of opposing colours.

81

THE AVANT-GARDE ERA

PAUL CÉZANNE (1839-1906)

Cézanne... 'A loner: a loner without chosing to be one, a loner in spite of himself', wrote Ramuz. Indeed. And, rather like Degas, he was at the very heart of the Impressionist group with which he only exhibited twice, in 1874 and in 1877. Renoir, Monet, Sisley and, above all, Camille Pissarro encouraged him to discover the light of the open air alongside them and, like them, to lighten his palette. This was a long process whereby he was obliged to undo his Romantic tendencies and, like all the others, shed the influence of museum art. The study of landscape, however, revealed this to him naturally: there he perceived nature's creative energy, he sensed its force. The world seen this way was no longer finite: it was a world in the process of being created, of being formed. 'I want to paint the world's virginity...' 'I wanted to discover the geological strata...' It was this perception of life in addition to the perception of the power that rules it that he wanted to try to convey in his painting. But how? The impressionist technique of the juxtaposition of colour becomes for him a crystallization which evokes the order of the landscape, that of the initial fixing of the elements. It is in the modulation of the different patches of colour alone, placed with a new and intense awareness, that he paints his picture, the idea of which is clear from the outset: 'Cézanne', writes Matisse, 'wanted his colours to be sources of power'; and Bonnard comments, 'Cézanne wanted each area of painting to be be of a conscious colour'. Each brushstroke of colour in each of his paintings has been premeditated, chosen and even calculated. The painter's vision has eliminated all detail and all ornamentation in order to leave only the essential.

82. 83. In this version of The Card Players *(c. 1890–1895, o/c 48.5 x 57 cm), Cézanne treats the human figure as any other motif, in the same way as his still lifes, one of his favourite subject matters. With* Apples and Oranges *(c. 1895–1900, o/c 74 x 93 cm), he overturns the traditional laws of perspective and arranges his objects according to their formal presence and their colour, as if he were painting an abstract composition.*

82

VINCENT VAN GOGH (1853-1890)

When he arrived in Paris from his native Holland at the end of February 1886, Van Gogh had already painted numerous works in sober tones with an intimist use of light. He had executed a great number of drawings of figures and landscapes (marshland, ponds, trees, roads in winter) which prefigure, in their diversity, his various styles of panting. He was already an admirer of Millet, whose themes he reused. Struck from the outset of his first stay in Paris by the works of the Impressionists - to whom he had been introduced by his brother Theo - he linked up primarily with Camille Pissarro, which led to the lightening of his palette and stylistic contrasts with his earlier period. The light is bright, the tones sustained. Then, influenced by Seurat, the brushstrokes became divided into tones grouped according to the law of complementary colours. He soon moved towards a simpler and more lively translation of colour, here following the example of his friends Emile Bernard and Louis Anquetin, who were inspired by the outlining of stained glass windows to delineate bright, flat areas of colour, and who particularly admired the 'extreme clarity' and the 'firm lines' of Japanese prints. It was in

83

79

84. 85. 86. The life and work of Vincent van Gogh are inseparable. If this portrait of Doctor Paul Gachet (1890, o/c 68 x 57 cm) is an expression of the artist's friendship, Bedroom at Arles *(1889, o/c 57.5 x 74 cm) expresses his anguish, while* Church at Auvers-sur-Oise *(1890, o/c 94 x 74.5 cm) is an hallucinatory vision of the small, tranquil village where the artist found refuge before shooting himself in the chest.*

February 1888 that Van Gogh left for the South of France. Once in Arles he was struck by the light of the sun: 'How beautiful the yellow is!' He was seized by a fever for work. Gauguin came to join him in October of the same year. Influenced for a while by the latter, Vincent painted *The Dance Hall*, happily now in Orsay. In it many of the Pont-Aven characteristics established by Bernard and Gauguin are visible: the flattening and outlining of planes of colour, the stylisation of the figures and their headgear and the schematisation of areas of light. But how could two such individuals see eye-to-eye for long? Stormy arguments followed and near Christmas came the drama of Van Gogh's cut ear. Each went his own way. Gauguin turned more and more towards nature with an imagination coloured by fable and myth, in search of an almost legendary art. Van Gogh knew that he could not bypass a reality which, with his acute sensitivity, he would render increasingly human. From this moment on, his colours become even stronger, he abandons the flutterings of Impressionism in favour of either vast monochrome areas or broad striations which give an object's form and colour simultaneously. He tends towards a light which is not only that of outdoors, but a light which is from the outset supernatural. He was in search of an ever more truthful expression of the mystery of man. In this quest for spirituality, he separated himself from Impressionism.

81

THE AVANT-GARDE ERA

NEO-IMPRESSIONISM

Neo-Impressionism, as its name indicates, is a new Impressionism, both its continuation and a reaction against it: continuation because like Impressionism it favours the open air, focuses on day-to-day life and uses a palette of light colours; reaction, because it replaces the intuitive technique of the juxtaposition of colour with a method of *division* of colour based on the scientific study of the relationship between colour and light. The movement was initiated by the young painter, Georges Seurat (1859-1891). When he began painting in 1878, Impressionism, then at its brilliant height, was already familiar to the public. Seurat too was dazzled by this explosion of light which gave him, like his friends from the École des Beaux-Arts, an 'unexpected and profound shock'. He quickly realised, however, how uncertain this impressionist technique could be. He spent the two years following his return from military service in 1880 devoting himself to drawing and produced a series of exquisite works in black conté crayon. Meanwhile, pursuing his love of precision and order, he read all the publications on optics and all the theoretical works on drawing and colour, numerous during this new scientific era. In its natural state a colour is affected both by the degree of light surrounding it and by neighbouring colours perceived simultaneously by the eye. Colour is the result of an optical mixing which takes place on the retina; it was thus a question of breaking down these elements, fixing them on the canvas in separated brushstrokes, and leaving the viewer's eye to reconstruct them. Seurat chose no longer to use mixed colours to this effect, as he was still doing in *Bathers at Asnières* (1884), but to use pure colours, as in *Grand-Jatte Island* (1886), 'a polychrome mass of small brushstrokes', as Félix Fénéon remarked. Paul Signac's name should immediately be associated with that of Seurat. His work *From Eugène Delacroix to Neo-Impressionism* is fundamental to the study of this movement. Other names that should be mentioned are those of Cross, Dubois-Pillet, Maximilien Luce, Théo van Rysselberghe and Henry van de Velde.

87. Paul Signac, The Red Buoy, *1885, o/c 81 x 65 cm/Signac has softened Seurat's systematic technique by increasing the size of brushstroke and reintroducing half-tones: the pinks and yellows of the small port of Saint-Tropez.*

88. Georges Seurat, The Circus, *1891, o/c 185.5 x 152.5 cm/ The artist's final masterpiece, left unfinished at his death. The formal and immobile character of his early works have been replaced by arabesques and movement rendered here by the warm colours–yellow and red–accentuated by the deep blue frame.*

87

88

90

GAUGUIN AND PONT-AVEN

'This school of Pont-Aven has stirred up as many ideas and influenced as many artists as the School of Fontainebleau in its day...' wrote Maurice Denis. Artists from America, England and Scandinavia were the first to discover, in the 1860s, the charming town of Pont-Aven in Finistère, Brittany. The place soon became known among the Parisian artists for its attractive countryside, the hospitality of its inhabitants and for the moderate prices of its boarding houses. Paul Gauguin settled there for the first time in July 1886; he soaked up the gentle climate and the soft, somewhat melancholy changing light outlining the hills and valleys, imbuing his art with a new spirituality. Leaving for Martinique in 1887, he returned to Brittany in February 1888. It was in this year the great encounters took place between Emile Bernard and Paul Sérusier. The young Bernard had already painted pictures using clearly outlined flat areas of colour. Gauguin, a friend of the Impressionists with whom he had exhibited since 1879, but an avid believer in the renewal of expression, was captivated by *Breton Women in a Green Meadow* by this twenty-year-old artist, which inspired him to paint, in his own style, *Vision after the Sermon*. If Emile Bernard's *Breton Women* constituted a dazzling manifestation of Synthetism and cloisonnism, Gauguin's *Vision* is an immense poem in which the imagination is left to take the lead.

Summer came to an end. A little while after the execution of these two paintings, the holidays were also over for Paul Sérusier, a pupil of the Julian Academy. But just before returning to Paris, he painted, 'under the guidance of Gauguin', a small landscape of the Bois d'Amour with schematised forms, pure colours and no modelling; a little painting which alone surpassed all the recent ideas and discoveries. On his return he showed it to a few of his Parisian friends, his closest friends, for whom this work was to become the 'Talisman'. Settled for a long time in Pont-Aven and then in Pouldu from 1889-1890, Gauguin was gradually surrounded by numerous other painters. They included Meyer de Haan, Filiger, Chamaillard, Jourdan, Maufra, Henry Moret, Slewinski, Willumsen and O'Conor. They all exchanged ideas based around one common goal: to paint from memory, to simplify and exalt the role of colour.

89. 90. Gauguin brought back Les Alyscamps *(1888, o/c 92 x 73 cm), a flamboyant demonstration of the possibilities of colour, from his stay in Arles with Van Gogh. The following year he painted* Self-portrait with Yellow Christ *(1889, o/c 38 x 46 cm), in which his face appears between a Christian image and the 'grimace' of a primitive-style ceramic.*

(see page 91)

89

85

91

92

93

91. Arearea (Joy), 1892,
o/c 75 x 94 cm.
92. Be Mysterious, 1890,
polychrome wood 73 x 95 cm.
93. Women of Tahiti or On the
Beach, 1891, o/c 69 x 91
cm/Paul Gauguin's art
reached its maturity in Tahiti,
which offered him numerous
new sources for inspiration. He
also made wooden sculpture
and became interested in all
forms of art.

94. The White Horse, 1898,
o/c 140 x 91.5 cm/This
painting, one of Gauguin's
last works, is also one
of his most enigmatic.

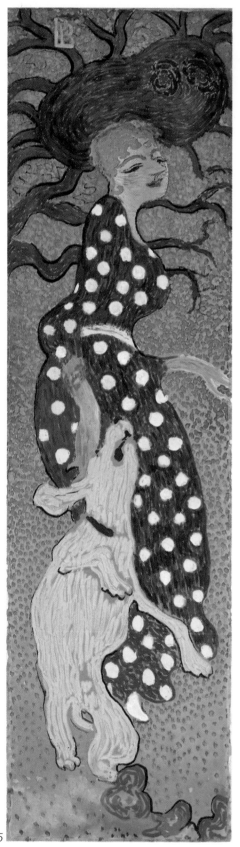

95

88

95. *Pierre Bonnard,* Women in the Garden, *1891, oil/paper glued onto canvas 160 x 48 cm.*

96

96. *Paul Sérusier,* The Talisman, *1888, oil/wood 27 x 22 cm/The Nabis assimilated numerous influences, from Gauguin, who 'dictated' Paul Sérusier's* Talisman, *to 'Japonisme', brilliantly reinterpreted by Bonnard, the most 'Japanese' Nabi, in* Women in the Garden.

97. *Félix Vallotton,* The Ball, *1899,* peinture à l'essence *and gouache on cardboard 49.5 x 61.9 cm/Gardens and children are among the recurrent themes of Nabi painting, treated here in an original manner by the Swiss artist, Félix Vallotton.*

98. *Edouard Vuillard,* In Bed, *1891, o/c 74 x 92 cm/ In this small masterpiece of concision, humour and observation, line alone translates the sense of abandon and depth of the dreamer's sleep.*

97

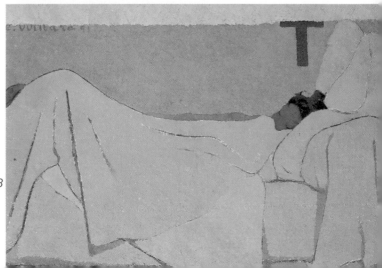

98

THE NABIS

The little landscape of the Bois d'Amour, painted by Paul Sérusier at Pont-Aven 'under the guidance of Gauguin' both stunned and captivated all the young artists from the Julian Academy and the École des Beaux-Arts to whom it was shown by Sérusier, their friend. Bright, almost pure colours, schematised forms; a striving towards extreme simplification; the panting was so different to those on show in the Salon, all adamantly realist works painted in a highly academic style. For they were unfamiliar with the Impressionists, those revolutionaries exhibited not in the Salon but in the Parisian galleries and known only to the initiated few. It was the Autumn of 1888. These young artists were Maurice Denis, Pierre Bonnard, Paul Ranson, Henri-Gabriel Ibels, Edouard Vuillard, Ker-Xavier Roussel and René Piot. Swept along by Sérusier, they were soon to discover the work of Gauguin and the paintings of the Impressionists. Academic subjects were finished; these canvases contained everyday life and above all, innumerable reflections of light. Suddenly, what freedom! Understanding its new meaning, they made the small landscape of the Bois d'Amour their Talisman. Having rediscovered Gauguin's works along with those by his friends from Pont-Aven in the Café Volpini, in the grounds of the Universal Exhibition in

99. Maurice Denis, The Muses, 1893, o/c 168 x 135 cm/ The flatness, the stylisation of forms and the sinuous line accentuate the decorative character of this composition reminiscent of the work of Puvis de Chavannes.

June 1889, they became the Prophets, *Nabis* in Hebrew, of the new gospel of painting. Their group, formed at this time, included foreign painters: Verkade, Rippl-Ronaï, Vallotton, Mogens Ballin. Together they quickly understood that the art of painting is to create a world in itself, a world distinct from nature. It is sufficient to compare any two artists from the group to see how different they were from one another - an indication of their freedom and abundantly creative spirit. 'Our merit, if there is such a thing, lies perhaps in the fact that we accept the most heterogeneous forms of expression as long as they are sincere', explained Vuillard. From Gauguin they retained the 'right to dare anything'; an audacity which is made manifest primarily in an originality of composition, the decorative stylisation of form, in the geometrical game of squares or checkered patterns, the bold use of colour and in the small format of these innovatory paintings, vast nevertheless in their scope. Highly aware of the social function of their profession, wishing 'to integrate art into life', they also explored all manner of decorative arts: first the entire interior of the house (wallpaper, fabrics, etc.) but then also the theatre, illustrations for books and journals, posters and prints. They spent ten intense years working together before finally going their separate ways.

100. Aristide Maillol, Mediterranean, 1905, marble 110 x 117 cm/The refined, simplified and monumental forms of Maillol's work prefigure a certain return to classicism which appeared in the 1920s and 1930s.

100

99

(see page 94)

ARISTIDE MAILLOL

There are certain timeless sculptures which in their form evoke plenitude and serenity. Such are the works of Maillol (1861-1944); they communicate strength imbued with gentleness. Maillol did not begin his training as a sculptor but as a painter. His four years at the Beaux-Arts allowed him to form a strong friendship with Bourdelle and to discover Rodin.

His admiration for the medieval tapestries in the Musée de Cluny and his association with the Nabis group led him to explore a new form of expression in tapestry. Gauguin encouraged him along this path. His first studies were already of young girls and female nudes. At the Universal Exhibition held in 1900, he discovered Egyptian and Indian statuary and from 1901 he exhibited his first sculptures at Vollard's gallery. Rodin admired him; he was diametrically opposed to him in his treatment of material but he had an extraordinary robust quality and was, above all, far from the servile imitation of academicism. André Gide supported him in the *Revue Blanche;* Octave Mirbeau bought some of his small works, and everything took off from there. He received his first official commission in 1905 for a monument to Auguste Blanqui. In 1908 he travelled to Italy and Greece. His sculpture then became 'archaic' with massive volumes and a rhythmical composition. Maillol created a new image of woman; strong and silent, grace and tranquillity incarnate.   I.H.

THE AVANT-GARDE ERA

EMILE-ANTOINE BOURDELLE

If there is any one sculptor who best expresses the passing from one century to the next, the real transition from Rodin to the avant-garde, it is probably Bourdelle (1861-1929).

His first official commission perfectly displays both Rodin's influence and the force of a more synthetic, massive sculpture. His statue *Monument to the Heroes of Tarn-et-Garonne, War of*

101. Antoine Bourdelle, Hercules the Bowman, 1909, bronze 248 x 247 cm/ Bourdelle's masterpiece perfectly expresses the energy and tension of the archer.

101

102. Henri de Toulouse-Lautrec, Dance at the Moulin-Rouge, 1895, o/c 298 x 316 cm/One of two large panels created for the house belonging to La Goulue, who is depicted here with Valentin 'the boneless' at the Foire du Trône in Paris.

worked together for fifteen years; Bourdelle, the craftsman, was responsible for finishing off works by the master.

'My art is the street, it is real life', announced Bourdelle. To this end he had inherited Rodin's analytical style with which he agreed, but he nevertheless continued to explore the expressive, unpredictable nature of his material, using strong contrasts between light and shade.

Looking at one of the huge warriors in *Monument to the Fallen at Montauban*, one can feel the tension through the body just as one can in the *Bourgeois of Calais*. Every part of the body is important to the overall expression and is treated in its own individual manner. Around 1900, Bourdelle felt the need to follow a more individual direction and it can be said that his first real work was his *Head of Apollo*. It too is expressive but the approach is new: the artist replaces the unfinished look with an impression of completion in his use of broad planes with distinct edges. *Hercules the Archer* (1909) is in the same style with its subtle interplay of volume and space. Although in three dimensions the bow can only be read from one angle. The work prefigures Bourdelle's mastery of bas-relief, especially those he would make for the Champs-Elysées Theatre in collaboration with the architect Auguste Perret. Bourdelle went beyond what he had learnt from Rodin and took part, alongside Maillol and Joseph Bernard, in the return to the 'Grand Style'.

1870, was inaugurated in 1902 after nine long years of research and of struggle against indifference or derision. Rodin was already successful enough and well-enough known to make this work accepted. A strong friendship existed between these two men who had

I.H.

93

HENRI DE TOULOUSE-LAUTREC (1864-1901)

Toulouse-Lautrec. The name alone evokes the numerous characters who were transformed by him into legends: cabaret singers, music-hall dancers, ladies of the night, clowns and acrobats, jockeys and circus amazons. Aside from some fine portraits of his family and friends, these were the favourite subjects of a painter who, like Degas, was an enemy of landscape. 'Landscape', he said, 'should serve no other purpose than to reveal the character of the sitter.'

In his early years, he was guided by the painter of animals, René Princeteau, then worked in Cormon's studio for several years. It was Degas, however, whom he admired above all, and who was his real master. Exactly thirty years separate them: Degas was born in 1834. The circumstances of their lives were very different: Degas led a hard-working life, one of solitude, devoted to his art. Lautrec's life was full of pleasure and torment and he detested being alone. They shared, however, the same sharpness of eye and of line, and although they were both, in their own way, skilful colourists, they were draughtsmen at heart. 'They both demanded a great deal of themselves', writes Henri Focillon, 'sharpening up a style which had become loose and unruly after half a century of experimentation.' Degas stands alone among the Impressionists. Following them, Lautrec made use of the freedom of their style, their striations, cross-hatchings and tones of woven colours; but he broke away with the force of his line, which, however brief, remains bold and precise. Even sketches by this virtuoso have a peremptory, finite character and an ever-present energy.   A. T.

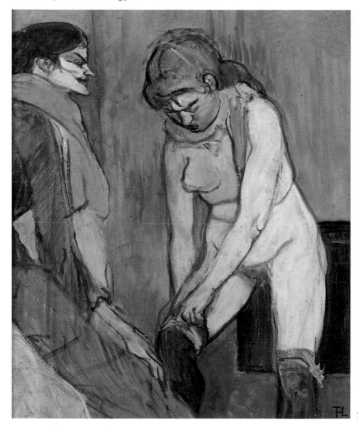

103. 104. Women, whether residents of brothels as in Woman pulling her Stocking *(1894, peinture à l'essence/ card 58 x 48 cm) or stars of the music-hall such as* The Lady Clown Cha-U-Kao *(1895, oil/card 64 x 49 cm), were Toulouse-Lautrec's favourite subject-matter.*

103

104

94

EXOTICISM AND SIMPLICITY

'May the love of Beauty and of Truth be your watchword in the struggle you undertake against the meanness and paganism of modern art and for the re-establishment of Catholic art in all its glory. I aus Deo', so A.W.N.Pugin proclaimed in the peroration to one of his first lectures at Saint Mary's Ascot college in the late 1830s. These lectures, which would be published under the title, 'The True Principles of Pointed or Christian Architecture', were one of the first of a series of manifestoes which would appear in Europe in the course of the nineteenth century, in the struggle against the opulent self-satisfaction of the century of industry. The invocation of truth and religion on the subject of architecture and interior design is characteristic of the speeches made by a young, twenty-nine-year-old man, trained at an early age by his father in the skill of ornamentation, and who, newly converted to Catholicism, confused with the same neophytic ardour his love for Gothic architecture and his hatred of industrial civilisation. Just as Viollet-le-Duc invoked a rationalist Middle Ages in defence of his vision of a modern, functionalist architecture, stripped of stylistic borrowings from the past, Pugin called upon pre-Reformation Catholicism in order to impose his vision of 'true' and 'honest' design on a century watched over by the false turpitudes of the new industrial processes and eclecticism. His 'True Principles' stoked the fervour of the English designers of the 'Arts and Crafts' movement and helped the majority of furniture de-signers (from Glasgow to Vienna, taking in Brussels and Darmstadt) to create the international Art Nouveau at the turn of the century. The 'principles' were ruthlessly simple and clear: 'The first rule of architecture is that it should have no element extraneous to the convenience, construction or function of the building. The second is that ornamentation should only be used in the embellishment of the essential construction.' In the course of his short but fertile life, Pugin was constantly refining simple, functional furniture, where possible in kit-form, designed for impecunious country priests. But, dogged by his manufacturers who were anxious to reach a wider and, above all, more wealthy clientele, he was obliged to embellish his most successful models with ornamental sculpture and (the ultimate sin) marquetry, models which were otherwise advertised, with an almost immodest honesty, for the simplicity of their construction. At the great Universal Exhibition of 1851 held at Crystal Palace, London, Pugin organised a vast 'Gothic court' where all the furniture and objects made according to his principles by his manufacturers Hardman, Crace and Minton, were on display. Alongside tabernacles or specifically religious gold and silverware, there were ceramic jardinières, wallpapers with brightly contrasting colours and fabrics and carpets which all brought to the public eye new decorative elements which had been created by Pugin and Barry during the building of the English Parliament. Ten years later, at the 1862 Exhibition in London, a second 'Gothic court' showed the fecundity of Pugin's principles and models in work by such names as Philip

From Pugin to Guimard, a whole line of designers, cabinet-makers and architects began to create furniture in 'new forms'. Inspired by the Middle Ages and Japan, this movement led to the development of Art Nouveau. By Jean-Louis Gaillemin.

105 Henri de Toulouse-Lautrec, At the New Circus, Papa Chrysanthemum, stained-glass window by L.C.Tiffany (120 x 85 cm), 1895/The work was commissioned by Samuel Bing on the occasion of the first Salon of Art Nouveau.

106. Three enamelled wares by Delaherche (1887, 1893 and 1899) on a pedestal table by Emile Gallé. On the wall, Odilon Redon, tree on yellow ground, decorative panel (249 x 185 cm) from the dining-room at Domecy chateau, 1901. This was Odilon Redon's first commission for decorative art which would be followed by work for Madame Chausson and the Fontfroide Abbey.

106

EXOTICISM AND SIMPLICITY

Webb, Richard Norman Shaw, William Burges and above all William Morris, whose name still symbolises the English Arts and Crafts movement today. Among the furniture exhibited by 'Morris, Marshall, Faulkner & Co.' was the King René study, its walls decorated by Ford Maddox Brown, Edward Burne-Jones and Dante Gabriele Rossetti. More eloquent than speeches, here was the symbol of the new alliance between art and craft preached by William Morris, a former theology student who had converted to architecture and painting. Using his generous private income, Morris tested the talent of his old friends from Oxford in the building and decoration of his own house (the 'Red House', built by Philip Webb in 1860) before starting up a firm which would make furniture, fabrics and wallpaper and create entire houses, continuing up until 1940. Even if Pugin's Catholicism had been replaced by militant socialism in Morris's anti-modernism, the Middle Ages, because of the social ideals it represented, still remained his own ideal. In fact, it was rich commissions from the 'artistic' fringe of this despised plutocracy ('I have spent my life providing repellent luxuries to the rich') which permitted Morris & Co. to finance simpler editions, destined in principle for the working classes. Gothic art would not, however, have succeeded in crystalising this long tradition of design which, paradoxically, would lead to the modern movement, if its development had not been stimulated by the totally a-historical but exotic example given by Japan. Only eight years after Japan had opened up to the Americans, the architect William Burgess, one of the most exuberant 'Gothic' designers of the 1862 Exhibition, drew attention to the existence, at the heart of the exhibition, of a 'Japanese court' which, he advised, should be visited daily by 'our students of the revival of thirteenth century art': 'It will not be time wasted since these barbarians who have remained unfamiliar to us until today, would appear to know all that was known in the Middle Ages; in some aspects they have even surpassed them, and us with them.'

Pre-industrial Japan symbolised the survival of the society of artists and craftsmen which until then had been situated, in the writings of Carlyle, Ruskin and Pugin, in medieval Europe. This unexpected alliance between Japan and the Middle Ages, forged by the avant-garde designers, found two eager followers in William Godwin and Christopher Dresser. The former with a touch of Ancient Greece, the latter with a hint of Egypt, they both created 'proto-modern' furniture and objects of rare elegance which were the delight of the most demanding of aesthetes. The houses in Tite street designed or decorated by Godwin around 1880 for the two promoters of fine interiors, James Whistler and Oscar Wilde, were clear examples of this exorbitant simplicity. When sending his cheque to Godwin, Wilde wrote, 'Each chair is a sonnet in ivory and the table a *chef d'oeuvre* in mother-of-pearl'. Whistler, who had told Théodore Duret: 'As you know, I attach as much importance to my interior decoration as to my paintings', launched himself into decoration and created the Peacock Room for his client Leyland where his *Princess with*

107

107. Emile Gallé, Hand with Seaweed and Sea-shells, *1904 (55 x 13 cm) / This was Gallé's last glass creation, presented in the year of his death at the exhibition of decorative arts at Nancy, along with a Squid Vase in a display cabinet* The Bottom of the Sea *with octopus-inspired legs.*

108. Vases by Emile Gallé presented in the Dragon-fly Display Cabinet *(230 x 130 x 60 cm), commissioned in 1897 by Henry Hirsch. Iron wood, oak lake, speckled mahogany, rosewood incrusted with mother-of-pearl and gemstones. With these zoomorphic feet, Gallé completely transformed his formal repertory.*

Peacocks reigned over an impressive collection of Japanese 'blue and white', the fashion for which had been launched in part by Whistler himself. In the 1880s the fashion for decoration enjoyed such success that it gave rise to numerous Arts and Crafts guilds and to the success of a perceptive merchant, Arthur Lasenby Liberty, who popularised the look in combining re-editions and new designs up until the First World War. Just as the Arts and Crafts network was beginning to decline, it produced its final designer, Charles Rennie Mackintosh, whose genius shocked the calm devotees of the movement but who enjoyed his great success on the continent in the international exhibitions held at the turn of the century.

The English influence on the European Art Nouveau cannot be overestimated. It was felt everywhere, from Glasgow to Vienna, through Brussels, Darmstadt and Munich and it is telling that the Italians refer to their Art Nouveau as *'Stile Liberty'*. When Henry Van de Velde decided to abandon painting in 1889 in favour of the decorative arts, it was the result of his enthusiastic reading of the English theoreticians along with a strong dose of Nietzsche. 'The work and influence of John Ruskin and William Morris were certainly the seeds that fertilised our imaginations, and especially our work, and provoked the total upheaval of ornamentation and form in the decorative arts.' The 'we' refers to the other protagonists of the Belgian Art Nouveau such as Hankar, Horta and Serrurier-Bovy who were all more or less content to follow the ideas of Viollet-le-Duc and his constructive rationalism. Van de Velde, like Godwin, was concerned with purity of line, the nature of the material and the reduction of ornamentation, all qualities which can be found in designs which date to just after Josef Maria Olbrich, Otto Wagner, Koloman Moser and Joseph Hoffman. As anglophile as they were lovers of things Japanese, the Viennese invited Charles Rennie Mackintosh to exhibit at the 1900 Secession and Adolf Loos redesigned, for the Austrian public, the famous 'Egyptian' three-legged stool sold by Liberty. The fact that the Austrians were so bold in their exploration of a purist path which gives their 'Art Nouveau' the premature look of 'Art Deco', is due to local circumstances. First, there was the existence in their history of an extremely purified neo-classical style known as 'Biedermeier', whose sobriety was asserted at the end of the century as an antidote to the pompous heavy official style. Secondly, there was the success of an industrial process, the technique for bending wood, invented by the firm Thonet in the 1840s, which led to the diffusion of the café chair (the famous *Number 14*) and the daring creations of the late nineteenth-century designers. Midway between London and Vienna lies Darmstadt, where at the instigation of the Grand Duke of Hesse, the Englishmen Baillie Scott and Ashbee were called upon to decorate two rooms in the Duke's palace, followed by the establishment of an artists' colony, the conception of which was left to the Viennese artist Olbrich.

It comes as a surprise that France should have remained relatively

109. François-Rupert Carabin, bookcase, 1889 (290 x 210 x 80 cm), walnut and iron cast by Albert Serval / This bookcase was commissioned from the artist by the engineer Henry Montandon. The importance of the sculpted elements and the exuberant metal ornamentation inspired by plant forms make this one of the most intriguing pieces of Art-Nouveau furniture.

110. Selection of Art-Nouveau chairs. From left to right: Majorelle, chair (100 x 40 x 40 cm), 1902–1908, in mahogany from Cuba. Henry van de Velde, pair of mahogany chairs (90 x 40 x 50 cm), 1896, and leather-covered oak chair from 1897 (90 x 40 x 50 cm).

110

109

EXOTICISM AND SIMPLICITY

isolated from this English-influenced European avant-garde, even if Viollet-le-Duc's Middle Ages and Japan were also catalysts in this country. The fault perhaps lies in the defeat of the Sudan which cut the French off from everything Eastern, and also in the fact that the new middle-classes remained attached to the revivals launched under the Second Empire, and there was no society of 'souls', like in England, who were sufficiently steeped in the new aesthetic principles to commission chateaux and houses from the new architects and decorators. Robert de Montesquiou's efforts to acclimatize to Paris the fragile flowers of the 'artistic movement' that he had discovered in London through his friend Whistler, are well known. But although the poet of 'The Bats' and 'Blue Hydrangeas' gave Sarah Bernhardt a few pieces of Lalique jewellery and patronised the celebrated glass-maker Gallé, who engraved some of his lines of poetry

111

onto his vases, he commissioned no more furniture after the completion of the 'Hydrangea' commode and the 'Clock of Thought', exhibited at the Salons of 1892 and 1894, and the Countess Greffuhle never commissioned the 'mysterious bedroom' from Gallé, which was perhaps intended for her daughter Elaine. Alone in this field was the original and self-assured collector, Countess Martine de Béhague, who commissioned Jean Dampt to make what is one of the most beautiful symbolist rooms in France. Certainly the 'École de Nancy' cabinet makers and designers might have appeared rather provincial to these distinguished collectors. The dining-rooms and bedrooms with mirror-wardrobes by Eugène Vallin and Jacques Gruber were not very far, under their floral disguise, from the Louis XV or Louis XVI interiors admired by the liberal middle-classes. Emile Gallé's attempts are typical of this organic dressing-up of traditional forms and neither the quality of the inlay work nor the lines of poetry, which were thought at the time to have been applied by pyrography, saved these models which, it must be said, were highly successful. Louis Majorelle, the only professional in the group, was in the habit of providing this type of furniture through catalogues, which led him to his most beautiful designs in this field like the 'Waterlily Furniture' which revives with brio, bronze gilt ornamentation on mahogany. In Paris, it was a foreigner, Samuel Bing, one of the promoters of *Japonisme* and international Art Nouveau, who recognised the most refined designers Eugène Gaillard and E.Colonna and above all Georges de Feure, who joined Tiffany and Van de Velde in the 'Gallery of Art Nouveau'. A place apart should be given to the architect Hector Guimard who was a late discoverer of Art Nouveau through Victor Horta. This patronage explains his Viollet-le-Duc-inspired taste for furniture with a visible structure, which his talent for design always enabled him to integrate into a coherent overall vision. Guimard's genius, refined over the years - his great masterpiece is in this respect his own house in avenue Mozart, built in 1912 - makes the mass of 'Art Nouveau' that took over the faubourg Saint-Antoine, the furniture district, immediately after the Universal Exhibition in 1900, seem all the more wretched in comparison.   J.-L. G.

111. Charles-Rennie Mackintosh, desk in white lacquered wood, 1904 / The highly stylized floral ornamentation of this Glaswegian designer strongly influenced the Viennese school and artists of the Wiener Werkstätte.

112. Alexandre Charpentier, panelling made for the dining-room (1901) in the house belonging to the banker Adrien Bénard in Champrosay (360 x 1050 x 620 cm), mahogany, oak and poplar / The fountain and the enamelled stoneware tiles are by the ceramist Alexandre Bigot. The gilt bronze decoration is by the firm L. Fontaine On the console is a table centre-piece by Raoul-François Larche, in zinc cast by Siot-Decauville (1894).

113. Koloman Moser, Paradise,
*1904, tempera on paper
415 x 774 cm (detail): an
archangel/A cartoon for the
stained-glass window on the
entrance portal of the Church
Saint-Leopold am Steinhof,
built by Otto Wagner between
1904 and 1907 near Vienna.
Both men were part of the
Viennese secession, an
Austrian version of Art
Nouveau, along with, amongst
others, Gustav Klimt.*

114. Louis-Charles Boileau,
Perspective View of the Interior
of a Church, *c. 1860–1865,
pen and gouache on paper/In
the 19th century, architecture
was also practised on paper,
and the tradition of the 'beau
rendu' was upheld at the
École des Beaux-Arts,
as is illustrated in this
imaginary view.*

HAUSSMANN'S PARIS

The name of Baron Haussmann remains inextricably linked to that of the French capital and it is impossible to speak of nineteenth-century Paris without emphasizing the work of the Prefect of the Seine under the Second Empire. From 1853 to 1870, Haussmann, following the wishes of Napoleon III, oversaw one of the most radical and rapid transformations that Paris has ever seen. Not only did he double its size by annexing seventeen neighbouring communes, but the Prefect transformed the face of the capital, now crossed by boulevards lined with regular rows of imposing six-story buildings. This urban and architectural upheaval was accompanied by a policy to modernize the various public supply systems, from the water supply to street lighting, right down to the sewers. Mention should also be made of the proliferation of the number of squares, the introduction of street furniture and the creation of the most beautiful Parisian parks, including the one at Buttes-Chaumont.   S.B.

113

The creation of a 'department of architecture' in the Musée d'Orsay seemed essential from the outset of the project: the building itself is a historical landmark, and more generally, architecture was a major art form of the second half of the nineteenth century and was at the centre of aesthetic debates of the time. Various schools opposed one another in these sometimes stormy discussions: partisans of eclecticism, such as Charles Garnier, fought against the upholders of 'rationalism' led by Viollet-le-Duc.

It was during this period that the metal architecture of Victor Baltard and Gustave Eiffel flourished; it is richly illustrated in the museum thanks to gifts made by members of the Granet family, descendants of the builder of the famous Eiffel Tower. Other

114

numerous and generous bequests have expanded the museum's collection of drawings, models and photographs: for example, there are Henry van de Velde's projects conceived during his Parisian period and an exceptional collection of moulds by Hector Guimard, representing the Art Nouveau movement in Belgium and France. Foreign architecture is also well represented: Koloman Moser's *Paradise* illustrates the Viennese secession, alongside examples from the Glasgow school–with Charles Rennie Mackintosh–or the Chicago school represented by Louis Henry Sullivan. A few very fine drawings by the American Frank Lloyd Wright make the link with twentieth-century architecture.   S. B.

PHOTOGRAPHY

The period from 1848–1914 was profoundly marked by the invention of a new medium: photography, a technique perfected in the mid-nineteenth century. It follows, therefore, that the Musée d'Orsay should have an large photography collection, something noticeably absent from other French museums. Today the collection numbers in the thousands, and is presented in a series of thematic exhibition dossiers, showing the diverse aspects of this discipline from its pioneers–Daguerre, Le Gay, Le Secq, Baldus–to the first modern photographers, with works by the American Alfred Stieglitz and his fellow countryman, Edward Steichen.

Photography revolutionized the world of arts, but above all it became a separate artistic discipline, just as painting or sculpture. The majority of these 'primitive' photographers, as Nadar referred to

115. Félix Nadar, Portrait of a Bare-breasted West-Indian Woman, *1854–1859, papier salé print from a collodion glass negative, on card/Félix Tournachon, called Nadar, developed photography as an independent art form: his portraits were often imitated by less talented photographers.*

116. Gustave Le Gray, Steam, *1857, albumin print on paper from a collodion glass negative/From the beginnings of photography certain artists like Le Gray were able to exploit the expressive possibilities of this new technique.*

115

them, had received an artistic training and used the possibilities of photography–framing, focus, intensity of light–in the same way as an engraver or a draughtsman, in order to translate an aesthetic sensibility. Whatever the subject–landscape, architecture, the human body, etc.–the photographer composed his subject. Apart from works by the well-known French names–including Atget, Marville, Nègre–the museum owns original prints by Lewis Carroll, J. Margaret Cameron, F. Evans and others. All styles are represented, from the pictorial realism of the 1880s to the Photo Secession at the turn of the century.　　　　　　　　S. B.

116

107

THE BOOKSHOP

There are three shops in the Musée d'Orsay offering a choice of books, postcards, posters and objects which cover the rich variety of artistic and cultural life in France and abroad from 1848 to 1914.

The bookshop is located in the former railway station buffet which has kept its splendid original interior decoration. It sells books in French and other languages covering the years 1848–1914. There are guides, catalogues of the collections, publications issued by the museum's cultural service as well as thousands of works covering all the artists active during this period: painters, architects, sculptors, decorators, musicians, writers, photographers and the pioneers of cinema. More than seven thousand titles are available to the reader, from the best-known books to the rarest catalogues, from current editions to precious facsimiles, all of which pay homage to the artistic creativity of the nineteenth century.

The postcard shop is located above the bookshop on a mezzanine level decorated with a frieze by Mucha for the 1900 Universal Exhibition. Reproductions in all sizes, calendars, slides and video-cassettes are all available.

The gift shop, decorated in 1991 in a welcoming and luxurious style which captures the charm of the nineteenth century, sells replicas of works in the museum made by contemporary artists: jewellery, sculpture, scarfs and engravings as well as *Les Objets dérobés,* a line of accessories and objects found in paintings in the museum collection. The visitor can take home Degas's absinth glass, Cézanne's

117

117. The museum booshop with Mucha's frieze.

118. Henri de Toulouse-Lautrec, Jane Avril Dancing, c. 1892, oil/card 85.5 x 45 cm/One of Toulouse-Lautrec's favourite models. He contributed to her fame with his posters.

Right: floor plan of the museum.

fruit bowl, Olympia's jewellery or even Marcel Proust's cattleya orchid.

Access to the bookshop and postcard shop from the quai Anatole France or from the museum for ticket-holders; to the gift shop from the square to the left of the museum entrance.

Opening times: from Tuesday to Sunday from 9.30 a.m. to 6.30 p.m.; Thursdays 9.30 a.m. to 9.30 p.m.

Additional services

- Frequent visitor card for the bookshop, postcard shop and gift shop.
- Catalogue of new arrivals in the bookshop: *Actualités de la librairie du Musée d'Orsay.*
- Make your purchases by telephone. Telephone: (1) 40 49 49 57.

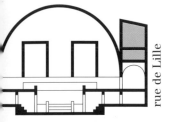

middle level

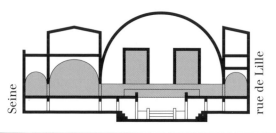

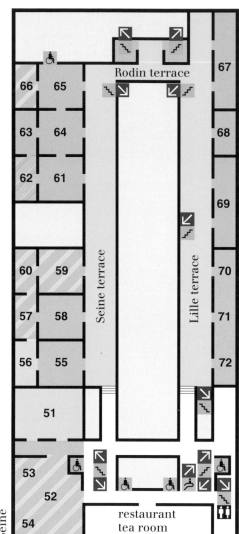

down to:
press corridor,
Kaganovitch
collection,
Dossier 5

ground floor

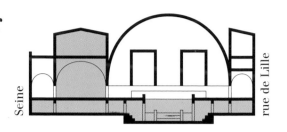

sculpture

- central aisle: sculpture 1840-1875, Carpeaux
- **2** Barye
- **4** Daumier

painting

- **1** Ingres and followers
- **2** Delacroix, Chassériau
- **3** history paintings and portraits 1850-1880
- **4** Daumier
- **5** Chauchard collection
- **6** Millet, Rousseau, Corot
- **7** Courbet
- **11** Puvis de Chavannes
- **12** Gustave Moreau
- **13** Degas before 1870
- **14** Manet before 1870
- **15** Fantin-Latour
- **16** open-air painting
- **17** pastels
- **18** Monet, Bazille, Renoir before 1870
- **19** Personnaz collection
- **20** Mollard collection
- **21** pastels
- **22** realism
- **23** orientalism

decorative arts

- **9** decorative arts,
- **10** 1850-1880

architecture

pavillon amont (alteration works under way) :
- **24** architecture
- **25** and furniture
- **26** from Viollet-le-Duc
- **27** to Frank Lloyd
- **28** Wright

M'O Dossiers

- **8** Dossier 1
- "Opera" room: Dossier 2

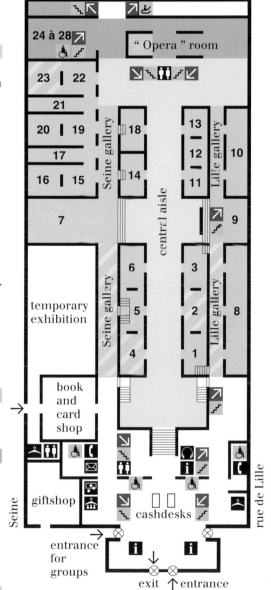

direct access to upper level

24 à 28

"Opera" room

23 | 22

21

20 | 19

17

16 | 15

Seine gallery

18

14

13

12

11

Lille gallery

10

7

central aisle

9

Seine gallery

6

5

4

3

2

1

Lille gallery

8

temporary exhibition

book and card shop

giftshop

cashdesks

rue de Lille

Seine

entrance for groups

exit ↑ entrance

Graphisme: C. Le Trung, C. Lebrun, F. Joffre 1994

upper level

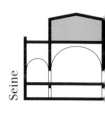

architecture

- **28** pavillon amont

peinture

impressionism and post-impressionism:
- **29** Moreau-Nélaton collection
- **30** Caillebotte, Whistler
- **31** Degas, Manet
- **32** Monet, Renoir, Pissarro, Sisley
- **34** Monet after 1880
- **35** Renoir after 1880
- **36** Cézanne
- **37** Degas (pastels)
- **38** Degas (pastels)
- **39** Van Gogh
- **40** pastels : Manet, Redon, Mondrian
- **41** Gachet collection
- **42** Le Douanier Rousseau
- **43** Pont-Aven school
- **44** Gauguin
- **45** Seurat
- **46** Signac, Cross
- **47** Toulouse-Lautrec
- **48** small paintings
- **50** Kaganovitch collection, level 4

sculpture

- **31** Degas
- **33** Degas, Renoir
- **44** Gauguin

M'O Dossiers

- **49** Dossier 5, level 4

28

29

30

31

32

33

34

35

36

open air terrace

Café des Hauteurs

37

38

39

41

40

41

Seine

PRACTICAL INFORMATION

Musée d'Orsay, 1, rue de Bellechasse, 75007 Paris, Telephone: (1) 40 49 48 14. Postal address: 62, rue de Lille, 75343 Paris cedex 07.

INFORMATION
Recorded message on (1) 45 49 11 11 and for groups on (1) 45 49 49 49. Information Desk: (1) 40 49 48 48. On Minitel: 36-15 Orsay or 36-15 Culture.

OPENING TIMES
Tuesday to Saturday, 10 a.m. to 6 p.m. (late night opening Thursday until 10 p.m). Sunday 9 a.m. to 6 p.m. From 20 June through 20 September the museum opens daily at 9 a.m.

GUIDED TOURS
French-language tours daily (except Sunday) at 11 a.m. and 2.30 p.m. and Thursdays at 7.30 p.m. English-language tours daily (except Sunday) at 11.30 a.m. and Thursdays at 7.30 p.m. Further details available from the Information Desk.

Besides the guided tours, the museum also offers educational activities (Young people's activity centre) as well as concerts, conferences, discussions and film projections (Auditorium, level 2).

MEMBERSHIP
The Carte Blanche is an annual membership which gives priority entrance to the museum and free entry to temporary exhibitions (further information on (1) 40 49 48 65).

SERVICES
Once inside the museum, visitors can enjoy the Restaurant on the Middle level and the Rooftop café (Upper level). A Bureau de Change, telephones and letter boxes are all available on the museum premises.

DOCUMENTATION ROOM
The public have access to a computerised information base, with images and texts, in the Documentation room (Salle de documentation) located on the mezzanine level of the Rooftop café (Café des hauteurs). Visitors can consult various programmes, by title, by author's name, etc. The museum's own publications and art films are also on open access and provide the essential complement to the computer programmes.

119. Claude Monet, La rue Montorgueil Decked out in Flags, *1878 o/c 81 x 50 cm / The 14 July through the eyes of Monet: a bouquet of colours where form is defined by the brushstroke, by-passing the drawing stage.*

CONNAISSANCE DES ARTS - Numéro hors série. **REDACTEUR EN CHEF:** Philip JODIDIO. **DIRECTION ARTISTIQUE:** Sylvie CHESNAY. **DIRECTION HORS SERIE:** Virginie de LA BATUT. **P.A.O.:** Alexis DUVAL, Bruno HERVIEUX, SERVANE RUAL. **SECRETARIAT DE REDACTION:** Françoise FOULON, Danielle MARTI.. **REDACTION:** Sylvie BLIN. **SERVICE PHOTOS:** Martine JOSSE. **SECRETARIAT:** Inès DUVAL, Monique FOUQUET, Kathryn LEVESQUE. **ONT COLLABORE A CE NUMERO:** Marina FERRETTI-BOCQUILLON, Jean-Louis GAILLEMIN, Isabelle HUSSON, Henri LOYRETTE, Caroline MATHIEU, Arlette SÉRULLAZ, Antoine TERRASSE. **DIRECTEUR TECHNIQUE:** Christian LECOCQ. **SERVICE COMMERCIAL:** Philippe THOMAS. **TRADUCTION:** Sophy THOMPSON.

CREDITS PHOTOS : Couverture et pages: 13, 14-15, 16, 17, 18, 19, 20, 21, 24, 34-35, 37, 38, 39, 41, 42, 43,, 44, 45, 46, 47, 48, 49, 50, 51, 52, 54, 55, 56, 57, 58, 59, 60, 61, 62, 63, 64, 65, 66, 68, 69, 70, 71, 72, 73, 75, 76-77, 78, 79, 80, 81, 82, 83, 85, 86, 88, 89, 90, 91, 92, 93, 94, 95, 96, 102, 104, 105, 106, 107, 109, 112, 114: RMN. P. 2, 4, 9, 13, 25, 26, 29, 30, 31, 32, 33, 53, 67, 97, 99, 100, 101, 102: Roger Guillemot/Bernard Saint-Genès. P. 4-5: Marc Loiseau/Archipress. P. 6-8: Roger Viollet. P. 7, 10, 11, 108: Didier Herman. P. 28, 29: Arnaud Carpentier. P. 23: Jacqueline Guillot. P. 84, 87: D.R. Droits réservés par l'ADAGP.

© 1995 Société Française de Promotion Artistique, 25 rue de Ponthieu, 75008 Paris. Tél. 43 59 62 00. R.C. Paris 75 B 4306 Seine. Direction de la publication: C. Lecocq. Commission paritaire : 55084 - ISSN 1242-9198. Dépôt légal: 2ème trimestre 1995. Imprimé par ISTRA-BL Strasbourg. Photogravure: Clin d'œil, Vanves et Cliché-Union, Montrouge.